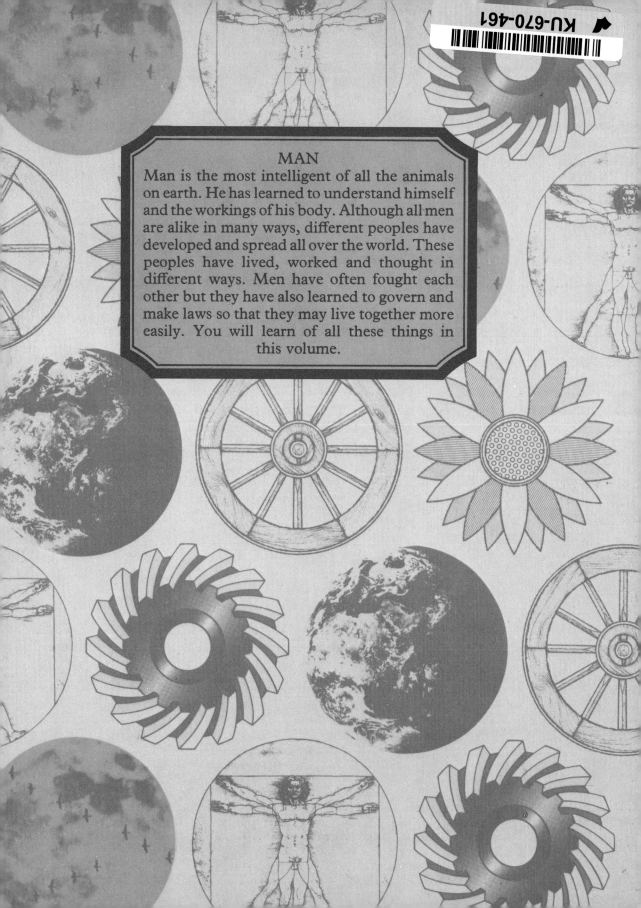

MAN

Man is the most intelligent of all the animals on earth. He has learned to understand himself and the workings of his body. Although all men are alike in many ways, different peoples have developed and spread all over the world. These peoples have lived, worked and thought in different ways. Men have often fought each other but they have also learned to govern and make laws so that they may live together more easily. You will learn of all these things in this volume.

OUR WORLD
ENCYCLOPEDIA
MACMILLAN

Volume 1

General Editor:
Leonard Sealey M. Ed.

Consultants
John Blackie C.B., M.A., Formerly
    H.M. Chief Inspector for Primary Schools
Professor Asa Briggs M.A., Vice Chancellor,
    University of Sussex
Professor Sir Bernard Lovell O.B.E., F.R.S.,
    Director of the Nuffield Radio
    Astronomy Laboratories, Jodrell Bank,
    Cheshire
Rosemary Sutcliff, Children's author

Advisers for Volume 1
Michael Chinery M.A.
A. R. Williams M.A.

Executive Editor
Philip M. Clark B.A.

Designers
Faulkner/Marks Partnership

Picture Researchers
Trisha Pike
Anne-Marie Ehrlich B.A.

Contributors
Neil Ardley B.Sc.
Dr Maurice Burton
Robert Burton M.A.
Kenneth Gatland F.R.A.S.
Peter Hildreth M.A.
Michael Hoyland
Josephine Kamm
Robin Kerrod
Geoffrey Trease
Ian Tribe B.Sc.

Artists
Terry Collins F.S.I.A.
Hatton Studios
Richard Hook
Illustrators London
David Jefferis
Eric Jewell
Ben Manchipp M.S.I.A.
Rodney Shackell
John Sibbick

© Macmillan Education Limited of London, 1974.
First published 1974
Reprinted with revisions 1975

SBN 333 14387 6 (Set)

Printed in Great Britain by W. S. Cowell Ltd, at the Butter Market, Ipswich

HOW TO USE THIS BOOK

Each volume of OUR WORLD covers a general subject. This volume is divided into the topics listed on the opposite page. If you are not sure which topic contains the information you need, turn to the index at the back of this book. If you need information from more than one volume, or if you are not sure which to look in, the Index Volume will help you.

Where a word appears in CAPITALS, this means that there is more information about this subject in OUR WORLD. If you cannot find it in the volume you are looking in, look the word up in the Index Volume. For example, you may read that 'The Egyptians studied the STARS'. This tells you that there is a section on Stars. The Index Volume will tell you that Stars are explained in The Earth and Beyond.

Sometimes a word is in capital letters even though it appears in a slightly different form from the heading.

MAN

All the parts of our body need to be kept strong and healthy. For example, we must have the right food for our BONES and TEETH to grow strong and hard. We have to have enough rest and sleep so that our BRAIN keeps active. Given the right amounts of food, rest, and exercise, our body will work well and provide us with plenty of energy.

Bones

Our bones form a skeleton or framework to support our whole body. Bone is a hard, whitish substance. Most bones are not solid but are slightly hollow. Inside is a fatty material called marrow. The marrow is important because this is where most of the BLOOD CELLS are made.

The main part of your skeleton is the spine. It is made up of 33 small bones or vertebrae. The spine is able to bend in all directions and also to twist. The largest bone in your body is the thigh bone. This is called the femur.

All your bones are different shapes and sizes. Some protect important and delicate parts of your body. The ribs protect your HEART and lungs and the skull protects your BRAIN.

When you are a child your bones are still growing and good food helps to make them strong.

Muscle

A muscle is a bundle of thick fleshy fibres in the body usually attached to a BONE. By pulling on the bones, muscles enable us to move. There are more than 600 muscles in the body.

Without muscles, it would not be possible to make any movement at all. Even the beating of the HEART is a muscular action.

Right: Muscle layers (in red) are cut away to show the bones.

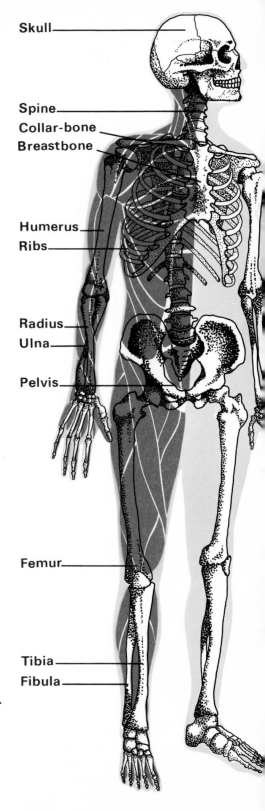

Skull

Spine

Collar-bone

Breastbone

Humerus

Ribs

Radius

Ulna

Pelvis

Femur

Tibia

Fibula

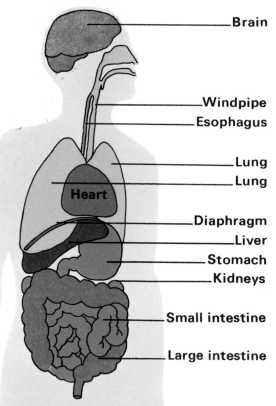

Brain

Windpipe

Esophagus

Lung

Lung

Heart

Diaphragm

Liver

Stomach

Kidneys

Small intestine

Large intestine

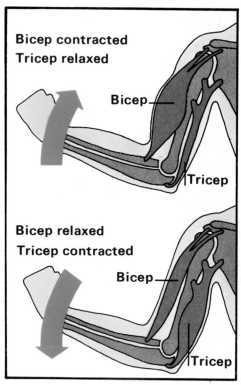

Bicep contracted
Tricep relaxed

Bicep

Tricep

Bicep relaxed
Tricep contracted

Bicep

Tricep

Above: The movements of the elbow.
Below: The inside of a bone (the humerus).

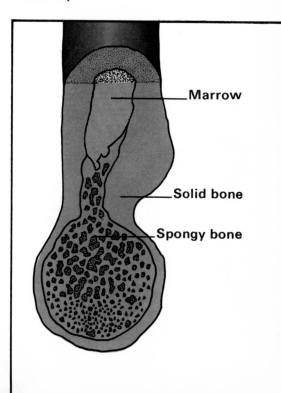

Marrow

Solid bone

Spongy bone

Blood

Blood is a red liquid which travels throughout the body. It is carried in tubes called veins and arteries. It takes with it the food and oxygen which keep the body alive and working properly.

The HEART pumps the blood round the body. Blood reaches every part of the body except the nails and HAIR. It is made up chiefly of a liquid called plasma. This contains the tiny red and white CELLS, which are called corpuscles. The red corpuscles give blood its colour. They also carry oxygen around the body. The white corpuscles attack any germs that may enter the body and help to destroy them.

If you cut your finger the blood starts to flow out. But it soon thickens or clots so that you do not lose too much blood. A healthy grown-up person has about six litres of blood in his body. If some of it is lost from an injury or illness, the body will make new blood to take its place.

Heart

The heart is a kind of PUMP which drives the BLOOD through the body. It is one of the most important parts of the body. If the heart stops working, death results.

The blood flows along the veins into the right side of the heart. From there it is pumped to the lungs where it takes in oxygen from the air. It comes back from the lungs into the left side of the heart. From there it is pumped into all parts of the body through the arteries.

Right: The blood system of the human body. The illustration shows only some of the blood vessels. Arteries are coloured red, veins are coloured blue. Inset: Red corpuscles in a drop of blood seen through a microscope. The white corpuscles are dyed purple, or they would be difficult to see.

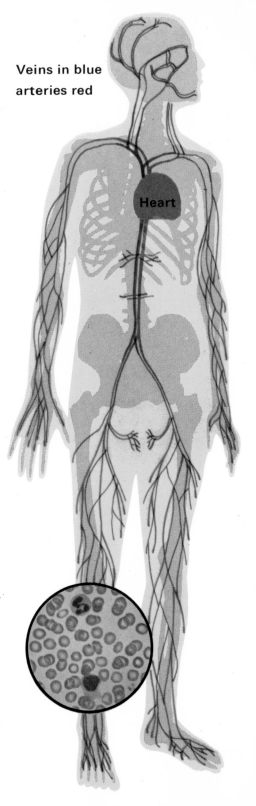

Veins in blue arteries red

Heart

The regular pumping of the heart is called a heart-beat. If we feel the pulse in our wrist, we can tell how fast our heart is beating. The heart of a child who is sitting still beats from 90 to 100 times a minute. An adult's heart beats from 70 to 80 times a minute.

If you are running about and playing hard, the body needs more food and oxygen. Then the heart beats faster, pumping the blood, with its food and oxygen, quickly through the body.

Right: The heart. A. Right auricle. B. Left auricle. C. Right ventricle. D. Left ventricle.
How the heart works. (1) The heart relaxes. Blood flows into the auricles. (2) The auricles squeeze the blood into the ventricles. (3) The blood is pumped round the body.

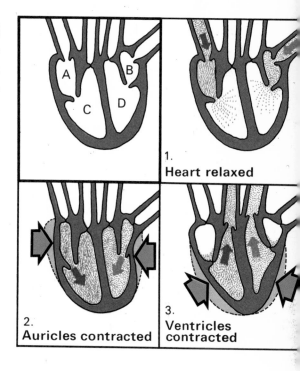

1. Heart relaxed
2. Auricles contracted
3. Ventricles contracted

Brain

Man has a better developed brain than any other animal. The brain controls almost every action made by the body. It is made up of millions of nerve CELLS and nerve fibres. These are surrounded by a fluid which protects them.

The brain is connected to the spinal cord, along which messages pass to and from other parts of the body. Each part of the brain controls a different activity. We know which areas of the brain control the senses, such as smell, taste, and sight. Another area of the brain governs speech.

In order to work properly, the brain requires oxygen from the air. This is carried to the brain by the blood system. Drugs and poisons affect the brain because they are carried to it by the BLOOD.

Different parts of the brain control different actions and functions. Some of these parts are shown.

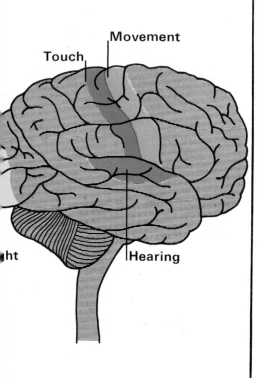

Movement
Touch
ht
Hearing

Skin

The whole of our body is covered by skin. In some places, such as the soles of our feet, it is very thick. In other places, like our eyelids, it is much thinner. The skin protects the body against injury and germs and also gives it information about changes in temperature.

The skin is divided into two regions. The outer region is made up of layers of dead CELLS. Underneath these protective cells there are thousands of sensitive cells. All over the skin are tiny openings called pores which give off unwanted fluids in the form of sweat.

Right: A block of skin, greatly magnified. The size of the hairs shows the scale of the diagram. The grease glands stop our skin from getting too dry. The tiny muscles can make our hair stand on end.

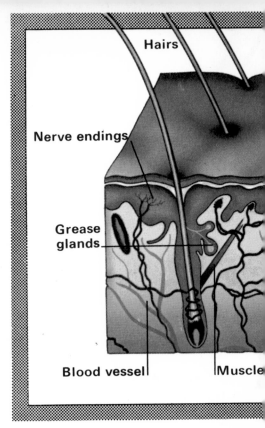

Cells

All living things are made up of tiny parts called cells. Our body consists of millions and millions of cells. Each cell takes in food and oxygen from the BLOOD, and each has a special job to do in the body. For example, the layers of SKIN cells help to protect the body: MUSCLE cells are long, and are sometimes striped.

Your nerve cells are very small, but out of them grow long nerve fibres. Messages travel along these fibres. Some fibres carry messages to the BRAIN, telling it what is going on. Other fibres carry messages from the brain, telling each part of the body to do a particular job.

Right: The cells in our body are many different shapes and sizes. (1) A bone-building cell. (2) A brain cell. (3) and (4) Cells at the back of the eye (the retina) which help us to see. (5) Long muscle cell. (6) Shorter muscle cell.

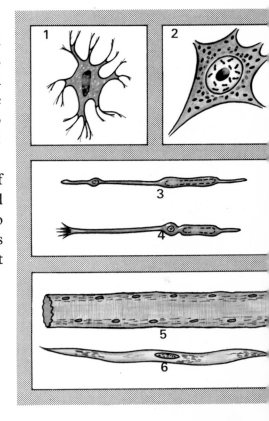

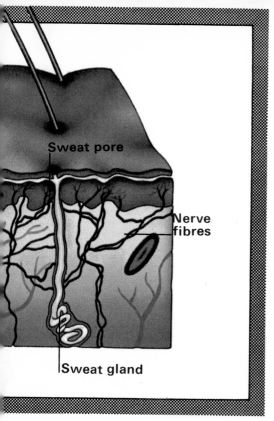

Sweat pore

Nerve fibres

Sweat gland

Hair

All MAMMALS have hair, though[...] than most. The hair of some mam[...] the form of fur, bristles, or even spines.

Hair grows on nearly every part of the human body. It is most noticeable, however, on the head. The hair on our head usually grows about 15 centimetres a year. If we did not cut our hair, it would probably not grow more than about 60 centimetres. This is because each hair then falls out. It is replaced by a new one, which grows up from a root in the surface of the SKIN.

The root of a hair grows in a space called a follicle. It is supplied with BLOOD from a tiny blood vessel. As new hair CELLS are made, they push the old cells upwards.

Our hair is actually made up of dead cells.

Glands

Any part of the body that releases a chemical substance is called a gland. For example, the saliva is made by glands in our mouth which helps us to swallow food.

Many glands make substances called hormones. These are often called chemical messengers. They are released into the BLOOD to reach all parts of the body and keep it working properly. The pituitary gland in the head makes a hormone which controls the growth of our body.

Lymph glands help to fight germs in the body. They produce cells which destroy BACTERIA. They swell up in the region of an infection. Lymph glands in the neck, for example, swell up when we have an infected throat.

The diagrams show the position of the main glands in men and women. Some experts do not consider that the liver is a true gland.

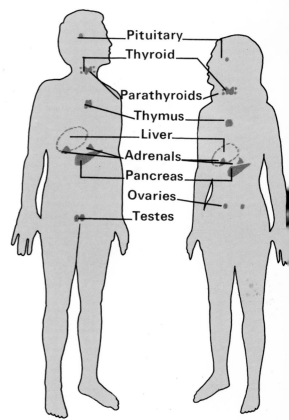

Pituitary
Thyroid
Parathyroids
Thymus
Liver
Adrenals
Pancreas
Ovaries
Testes

Breathing

When we are sitting still we breathe in and out about sixteen times every minute. The air that we take in through the nose or mouth goes down the windpipe and into our lungs. Our lungs are like two large balloons inside the chest. They swell up when the air flows into them.

The surface of the lungs is covered with tiny blood vessels. Oxygen, a gas which makes up about one-fifth of the air, passes through the lung walls and into the BLOOD. It is then carried through the body in the bloodstream.

Oxygen is essential for life. We use it to burn

Right: The main organs with which we breathe. Alveoli are tiny branching tubes. Through these, oxygen gets from the lungs into the bloodstream. Below: We use our ribs and diaphragm for breathing. To breathe in, we expand our rib cage.

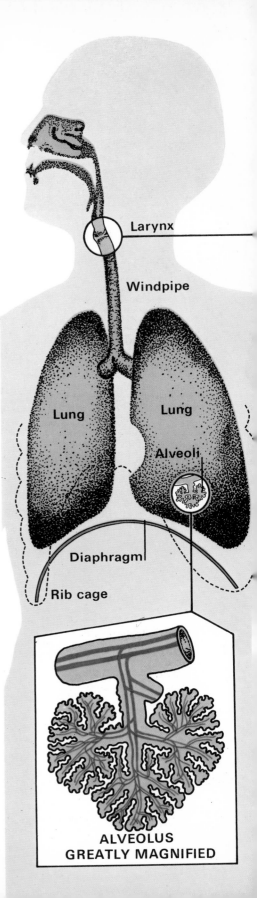

Larynx

Windpipe

Lung

Lung

Alveoli

Diaphragm

Rib cage

ALVEOLUS
GREATLY MAGNIFIED

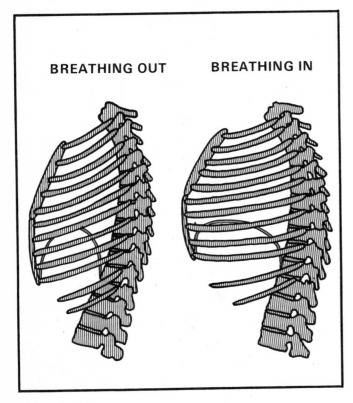

BREATHING OUT   BREATHING IN

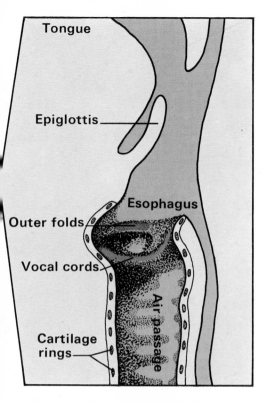

up food to keep us warm and to give us energy for moving. When we run about we need more energy than when we are sitting still, and so we need more oxygen. We breathe more quickly when we are running – perhaps as much as fifty times every minute. Burning the food in our bodies produces another gas called carbon dioxide. The blood carries this back to the lungs and we breathe it out.

We do not have to think about breathing because we do it automatically. The BRAIN sends signals to the chest, telling it how often to breathe in and out.

Left: The voice box, or larynx. The vocal cords are shown in red. The windpipe has rings of cartilage, which act as stiffeners. The epiglottis seals off the windpipe when we are eating. Otherwise we would choke.
The 'false vocal cords' are shown in green. They were once thought to be proper vocal cords.

Talking

As soon as a baby is a year or two old it begins to talk. Talking is the main way in which we can understand each other.

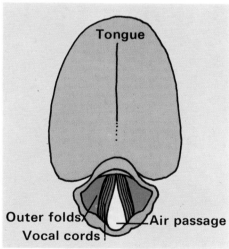

The sounds we make when we talk are first formed in our voice box. When we breathe out, the air is forced out of the lungs and up through the windpipe. Then it passes through the voice box. Here are two little MUSCLES called vocal cords which vibrate and make sounds. Our tongue, mouth, and lips all help to change the sounds so that they come out as different words.

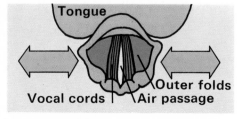

The organs of speech, seen from above. (1) Vocal cords open. (2) Vocal cords partly closed. Sound is produced by the rapid opening and closing (vibration) of the vocal cords.

Eating

The food we eat helps to give us energy. It has a long journey before all its goodness has been taken into our body.

When we put food into our mouth, it is first broken up by the TEETH, with the help of saliva. It then passes down the gullet and into the stomach, where it is turned over and over. Digestive juices from the stomach wall help to break it down into a thick liquid. The food takes up to six hours to be digested in the stomach, depending on the size of the meal.

After it leaves the stomach, the food goes into the small intestine, a coiled tube almost 7 metres long. More digestive juices are added here and the food is broken down still more. All the goodness from it passes into the BLOOD through the walls of the intestine. The blood carries it to the CELLS of the body to nourish them.

Any undigested food passes into the large intestine. This tube is wider than the small intestine, but not as long. From here it passes out of the body.

Right: The human digestive system.
Below: The salivary glands. There are actually six of these glands, three on each side of the face. A grown-up produces about a litre of saliva each day.

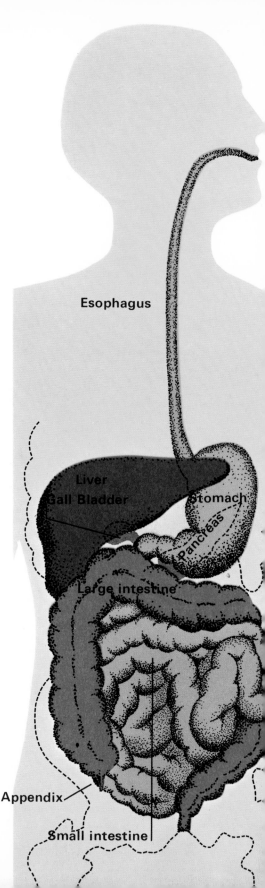

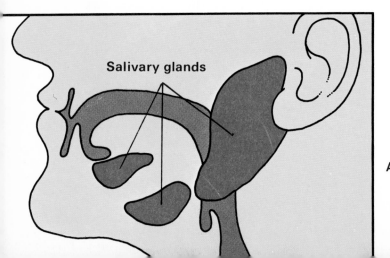

Teeth

Most children are born without teeth. At first they do not need food that has to be chewed. At the age of about eight months the first teeth appear through the gums. These first or 'milk' teeth are soon lost. By the time you are about 14 you should have nearly all your permanent teeth.

A root holds each tooth into the jawbone. You cannot see these roots because they are hidden by the gums. The hard white part that you can see in the mouth is called the crown. Inside the crown is a thick layer of strong material called dentine. The centre of the tooth is made of pulp, which is softer. The pulp contains the nerves, and it is through these that you feel the pain of toothache.

Holes (caries) in the teeth are caused by food becoming caught between the teeth. Food forms an acid which destroys the crown, and the pulp is then attacked by BACTERIA.

Regular brushing and visits to the dentist help to keep your teeth strong and healthy.

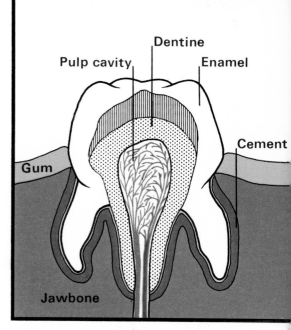

Above: The inside of a molar, or back tooth. The roots hold the tooth into the jawbone. A layer of cement around the roots helps to keep the tooth in place.

Sleeping and Dreaming

Everyone needs sleep so that their bodies can make up the energy used in the day. Growth takes place mainly when we are asleep. Children need more sleep than grown-ups because they are still growing. New-born babies sleep nearly all the time except when they are being fed.

Although we are not conscious of anything when we are asleep, sometimes we dream. When we dream we imagine that we are awake. Often strange things seem to be happening to us. Dreams are a mixture of our fears and hopes and what we have done and thought.

This painting, by D. G. Rossetti, has a strange dream-like atmosphere.

Birth

Life goes on because living things produce other living things like themselves. This is called reproduction. Birds and many other animals, for example, lay eggs from which the young hatch.

There are many animals, including humans, in which the baby grows inside the mother's body. In human beings this process takes nine months. The baby receives its food from its mother's bloodstream. At the end of the nine months the baby is born. At first it is helpless and has to be looked after by its mother.

Left: This child's mother is pregnant, and will soon have another baby.
Below left: The development of a baby before it is born.

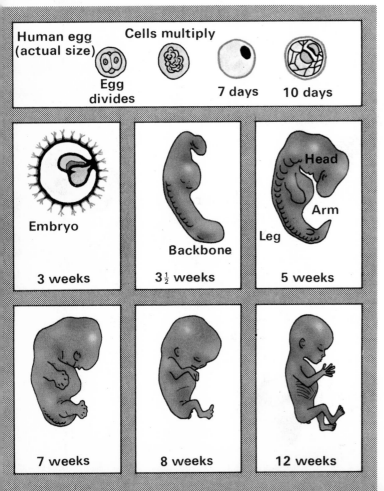

Human egg (actual size)   Cells multiply

Egg divides   7 days   10 days

Embryo
3 weeks

Backbone
3½ weeks

Head
Arm
Leg
5 weeks

7 weeks

8 weeks

12 weeks

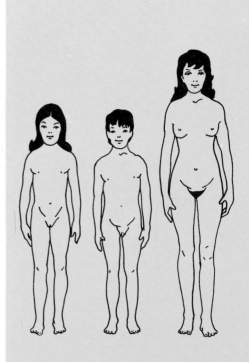

About 9 years (before puberty)   About 14 years (puberty)

Heredity

We expect a lion and lioness to produce a lion cub and not a baby monkey. In the same way, we expect a human baby to grow up like its parents. A child may have brown eyes like its mother and fair HAIR like its father. The child inherits these things from its parents. Many features may be handed on from generation to generation. We call this heredity.

Often there is a gap in heredity. A child may not look like his parents, but he may look like his great-grandfather. Some of the ways in which people behave may also be inherited.

At one time the Hapsburgs were the most powerful family in Europe. Charles II (right) and Philip IV (far right) of Spain both had Hapsburg features.

Growing

Much of the food we eat is used to give us energy. Some of it, however, goes to build BONES and flesh. In other words, it helps to make us grow. The speed at which we grow depends upon certain GLANDS in the body. These glands make hormones which control the rate at which we use our food.

We do not grow steadily all the time. A young baby grows very rapidly for a few months. Then its rate of growth slows down. The rate of growth speeds up again between the ages of eleven and fourteen, when boys and girls start to change into men and women. Girls usually start to grow before boys. They are often taller than boys for a while. But the boys usually overtake them later. Most people stop growing altogether when they are about twenty years old.

About 20 years
(after puberty)

Left: The average size of boys and girls at different ages.

The Five Senses

The five senses are: hearing, sight, touch, smell, and taste. A sound is first caught by the outer ear (the part you can see) and is directed down a canal to the eardrum. The eardrum vibrates when the sound hits it. The vibrations are then magnified by three little BONES in the middle ear. They carry the sound to very sensitive nerves which pass the sound on to the BRAIN.

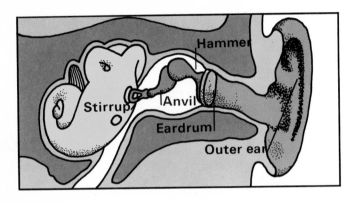

Light goes into the eye through the pupil. The coloured ring (iris) around the pupil lets in the right amount of light. What we see is focused (made clearer) by the lens, and is recorded on the retina at the back of the eye. The optic nerve then carries the picture to the brain.

We have many little sensitive spots on our SKIN. They give us a sense of touch. They let us feel things. We can feel whether something is

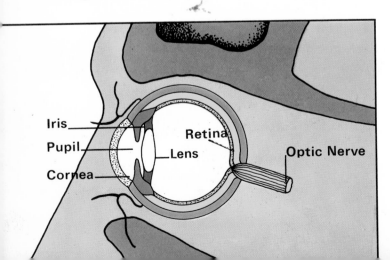

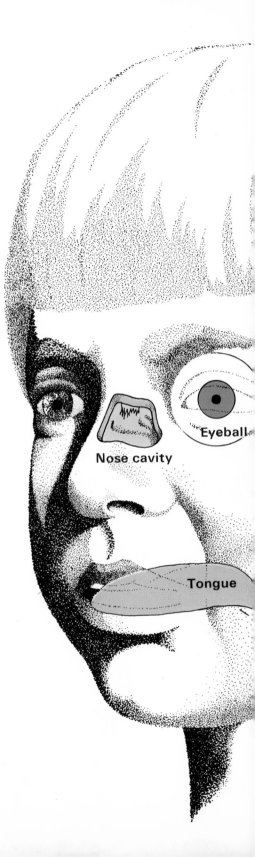

smooth or rough, wet or dry, or hot or cold. The touch spots are more numerous in some parts of our body than in others.

Many substances give off a scent or smell. The smell consists of millions of tiny particles which float in the air. We use our noses to detect them. When we smell a flower or a piece of cheese, for example, the particles are drawn up the nose to the smell CELLS in the upper parts of the nose.

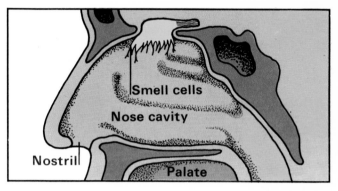

The smell cells tell the brain what kinds of particles they are.

A lot of what we think of as 'taste' is in fact smell. We actually smell and taste food at the same time. We taste things with groups of cells, or 'buds' on the tongue. (Children have them on the palate as well.) There are four main tastes: salt, sour, sweet, and bitter. The diagram shows where the buds are found for the different tastes.

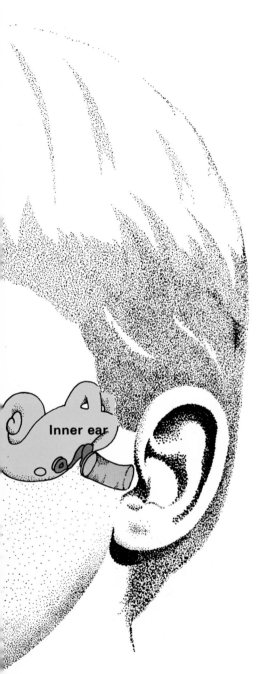

A child's head, showing the position of the sense organs. The inner ear is greatly enlarged. It is actually only a few millimetres across.

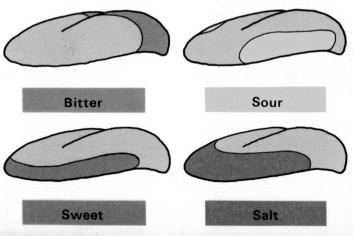

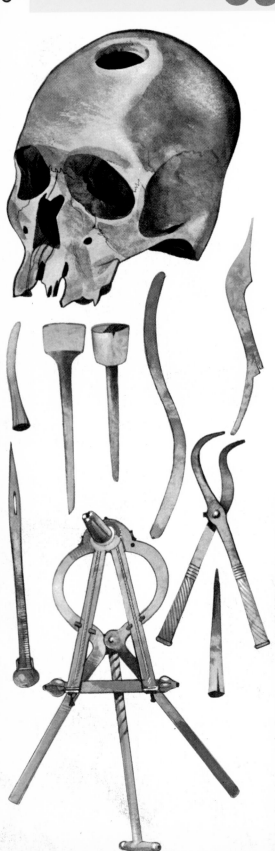

From the beginning of history man has suffered from many diseases and has searched for ways to cure them. Primitive man used herbs and berries when he felt ill, or he tried to cure himself by using MAGIC.

The ANCIENT EGYPTIANS studied medicine, and their priests acted as doctors. Later, in ANCIENT GREECE, a scholar named Hippocrates taught the art of healing. When his pupils became doctors they made a solemn promise to help the sick. This promise is called the Hippocratic Oath.

About 200 years ago doctors began to understand how the body works. This knowledge helped them to understand and cure diseases.

Above left: Many Stone Age skulls have been found with holes bored in them.
Below left: Ancient Roman surgical instruments. They are made of bronze.
Below: Medicine in fifteenth-century Italy.

A part of the body is diseased when it is not working properly or is affected by BACTERIA or VIRUSES. Today, modern science is successfully preventing and curing many diseases by the use of vaccines or DRUGS. Diseases such as smallpox, diphtheria, and tuberculosis are far less common now. But there are still some diseases for which scientists have not yet found a cure.

The lack of some kinds of food can cause diseases such as scurvy or rickets. Some people get occupational diseases from working with poisonous substances or in difficult conditions. There are also many kinds of mental diseases that affect the way people think and act.

Top right: A patient in a modern hospital being shown how to use a wheelchair.
Centre right: This patient is breathing with the help of a respirator.
Below right: Nursing in the nineteenth century. The nurse is wearing a very formal uniform.

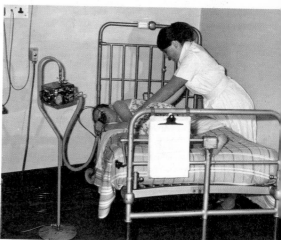

Surgery

Surgery consists of operations in which part of the body is repaired or cut away. Stone Age man carried out surgical operations using sharp flints. Scientists have found skulls with holes bored in them, though they do not know exactly why this was done.

Until recently surgery was very dangerous. The patient had to put up with the pain and he often died because the wound became poisoned. In modern surgery the patient is put to sleep with a chemical called an anaesthetic, so that he feels no pain. The operating theatre is kept spotlessly clean. The surgeons and nurses scrub their hands and wear masks. Every care is taken to prevent BACTERIA getting into the wounds.

Right: An operation on the ear in 1524.
Below left: A painting by Rembrandt of an anatomy lesson in the seventeenth century.
Below right: A modern operating theatre.

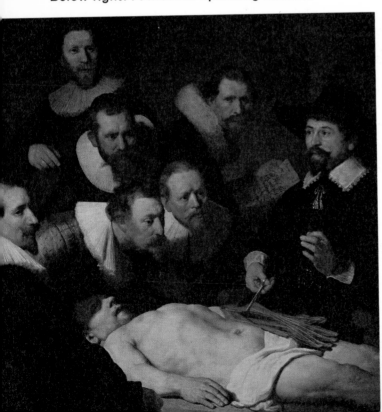

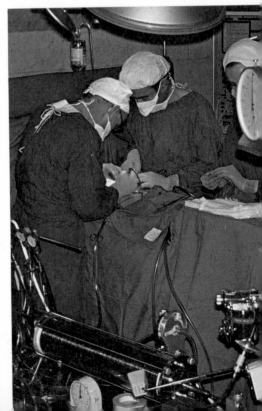

Surgeons use knives called scalpels to remove a diseased part of the body. They sew the cut edges together again with catgut, which is made from sheep's intestines. Operations on SKIN, MUSCLE, and BONE are sometimes quite simple. BRAIN and HEART surgery are much more difficult, but even parts of the brain can be removed.

It is now sometimes possible to replace a diseased part of the body. New bone joints can be made from metal or plastic. Sometimes the new part is taken from a dead person. This process is called 'transplant' surgery. The first transplant of a human heart, where the patient lived for several weeks, took place in 1968.

Dentistry

Over 100 years ago there were few dentists. When a person had bad TEETH, he went to a blacksmith or a barber to have them pulled out. Today, however, dentistry is a science. A dentist must study for up to six years. He must know how teeth grow, how they are made, and what makes them go bad or decay. He must be able to repair decayed teeth and know how to make dentures (false teeth). A modern branch of dentistry is correcting uneven teeth, which can spoil a person's looks, and may make EATING difficult.

The equipment that dentists use is improving all the time. Modern high-speed drills make work much faster. New materials are being developed for filling holes in decayed teeth.

Dentists try to maintain our teeth in good repair so that we can keep them for as long as possible.

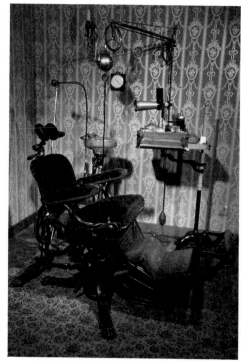

Above: A dentist's surgery of 1900. Painless dentistry was just being introduced.

Right: A dentist examines a patient in a modern surgery. Compare this picture with the one above it.

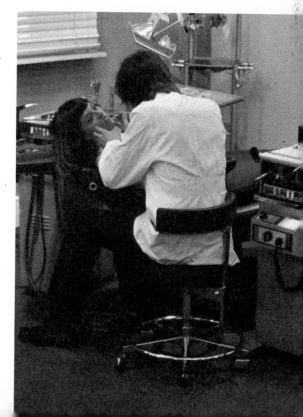

Virus

A virus is a tiny creature, often called a germ or 'bug'. They are smaller than BACTERIA.

Viruses can grow and multiply and cause DISEASES. Smallpox, measles, the common cold, and many other illnesses are caused by viruses. Some of these diseases, such as smallpox, can be successfully prevented by vaccines. Some can be treated with DRUGS. Others are more difficult to overcome. Even today, in spite of 50 years of research, there is no known cure for the common cold.

Viruses are the cause of many diseases in animals, such as foot-and-mouth disease in CATTLE. They also cause a number of plant diseases.

Right: Viruses usually have regular shapes.

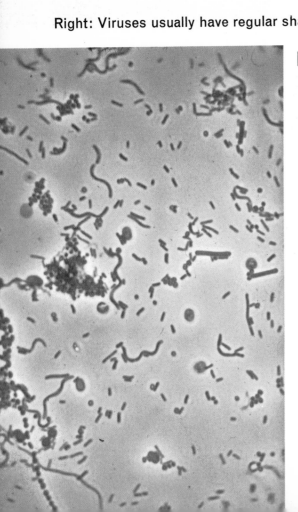

Bacteria

Bacteria are creatures so tiny that they can only be seen under a very strong MICROSCOPE. They live in the SOIL, in the sea and in the air. When anything rots or goes bad, it is probably due to bacteria. Some bacteria invade our bodies and cause diseases, such as typhoid fever, and tuberculosis.

Today vaccines are used to help the body fight bacteria. DRUGS such as penicillin are also used to kill them when they get inside the body.

Some bacteria are useful in industry. For example, some NATURAL FIBRES, such as flax, can be separated by the action of bacteria. The treatment of sewage also relies on bacteria.

Left: A photograph of bacteria, taken through a microscope. Bacteria are very small, but they are larger than viruses. Many diseases are caused by the action of bacteria.

X-Rays

If any part of the body is placed between X-rays
and a fluorescent screen, a shadow picture of the
BONES appears on the screen. If this picture is
projected on to a photographic plate, the result
is an X-ray photograph (or radiograph). Doctors
use X-rays to examine bones or other parts of the
body we cannot normally see. X-rays can also
help to cure certain skin diseases, and cancer.

Too great an exposure to X-rays can be
dangerous, however. Great care needs to be
taken to avoid damage to healthy CELLS.

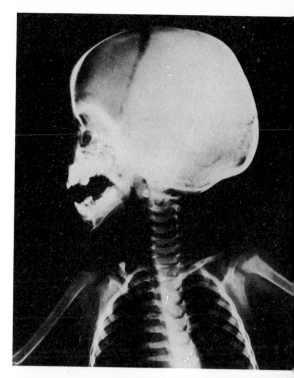

Right: An X-ray of a child's head and chest.
This child is suffering from a serious disease
called spina bifida, which has enlarged its skull.
X-rays were discovered accidentally by Wilhelm
Röntgen in 1895.

Vitamins

Vitamins are chemical substances found in very
small quantities in most foods. They are necessary for good health and normal growth of the
body. They were first discovered in 1911.

They are often called by letters of the
ALPHABET. For example, vitamin A is important
for growing, and is found in carrots, butter, and
eggs. Vitamin B, a mixture of several vitamins,
is found in many different kinds of food. The
body cannot work properly without it.

Vitamin C is contained in fresh fruit and
vegetables. In the past, sailors sometimes got a
disease called scurvy because their food contained no vitamin C. Doctors then discovered
that drinking fruit juice prevented this happening. Vitamin D helps the growth of BONES and
TEETH.

Some of the main food sources of vitamins.

A group of people having the same skin colour, shape of head, and type of hair is called a race. Scientists divide the peoples of the world into five different races. Most people belong to the three main ones which are: WHITE-SKINNED, BLACK-SKINNED, and YELLOW-SKINNED. Two smaller races are the Australian ABORIGINES and the BUSHMEN of Southern Africa.

There is no such thing as a 'pure' race. Men often marry women of another race and their children may show a mixture of features. People of the same race may live in different countries, and have different languages and customs.

Left: Arabs, such as this girl from Morocco, belong to the white-skinned group of peoples.
Below: A group of students from several races.

Aborigines

'Aborigines' are the first or 'original' dwellers in a country before others came and took over their land.

Today the word is used mainly of the Australian aborigines. They are tall, wiry, dark-skinned people with black curly HAIR. Some still live a hard, primitive life, wandering through the bush. They hunt game with spears or a curved wooden boomerang. Others work on farms and are very good at handling horses and CATTLE. There are far fewer aborigines today than there were when the first white settlers arrived in Australia two hundred years ago.

Left: An aborigine dance, in which the dancers imitate the movements of an Australian bird.

Bushmen

The Bushmen were the first people to live in Southern AFRICA. They live in family groups which come together during the rainy season in bands and scatter in the dry season when the game disperses. They are expert hunters and kill the game with poisoned arrows and other primitive weapons. They live on game, bulbs and roots, insects, and other creatures such as FROGS.

Bushmen are very short, with yellow-brown skins, long low skulls, and big cheekbones. They are unlike the various black peoples of Africa, so they are classed in a racial group by themselves.

There are now only about twenty thousand Bushmen left in the Kalahari region.

Right: A family of bushmen in the Kalahari desert. One of them is trying to coax a flame out of some ashes.

White-skinned Peoples

The peoples we call 'white' are really either pink or pale brown. They vary greatly in type. Their HAIR may be of any shade from blond to black. Their eyes may be brown, blue, grey, or green. They may be tall or short. Their skulls may be long or round. They may be tall, fair-haired Danes or shorter, olive-skinned Italians. They could also be darker-skinned ARABS, Indians, or Pakistanis.

We cannot say what a typical white man looks like. We can only say what he does not look like. If the colour of his skin does not help us, we can look for the features which would mark him clearly as a member of another race. He may have the kind of lips and hair that go with black people or the nose and eyes of the yellow people.

The white-skinned peoples are not only those who live in EUROPE or have left Europe to settle in other lands. They are spread all along North AFRICA and the Middle East, and include many of the people of Central ASIA.

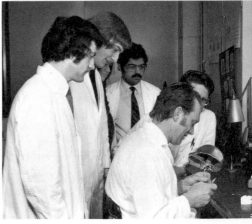

Top: This Arab girl has a very pale skin.
Right: These dental students are all white-skinned, including the Indian at the back of the group.

Area first inhabited by white-skinned peoples

Black-skinned Peoples

The black race is made up of the black Africans, and of other peoples living in Papua, Melanesia, and nearby lands of South-East ASIA. In the past (early sixteenth to early nineteenth centuries) many blacks were captured and sent to America to work as slaves.

Today, long after the slave-trade was stopped, there are about 15 million black people in the United States. There are also many in BRAZIL and other parts of the American continent. Some have now moved from the West Indies to Britain.

Like the white-skinned peoples, blacks vary in many ways. Their skin may be any shade of brown or black. Some are very tall. Some, like the Congo pygmies, are very small. Many have short, woolly black hair, broad lips, and a wide nose. Outside AFRICA there has been more inter-breeding with other races and some of these features may not be so marked.

Top right: This girl student comes from Nigeria, in western Africa. She has features typical of the black-skinned race. These include woolly hair, broad lips, and a wide nose.
Right: A black missionary reads to some children.

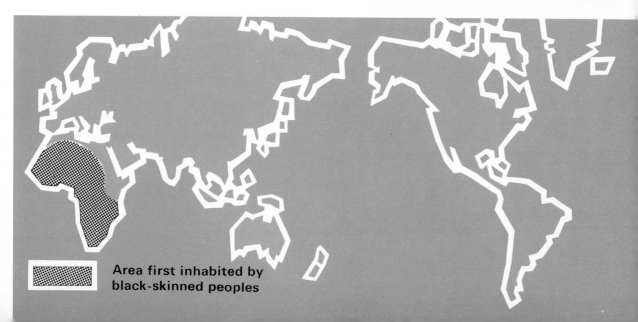

Area first inhabited by black-skinned peoples

Yellow-skinned Peoples

The yellow race is often called the Mongolian or Mongoloid race because its special features are those of the Mongol peoples of Central ASIA. These features are a yellowish skin, high cheek-bones, straight black hair, a flattish nose, and a slant-eyed look, caused by a fold of skin at the inner corner of the eye.

The map shows how the other yellow-skinned peoples spread out from Mongolia to occupy other countries: CHINA, Tibet, KOREA, JAPAN, and the nations of South-East Asia. They also crossed the narrow Bering Strait into NORTH AMERICA.

The original inhabitants of Siberia were also Mongolian in type. So are the LAPPS who live today in the far north of FINLAND, SWEDEN, and NORWAY, and so are the ESKIMOS. AMERICAN IN-DIANS come from this same stock, though their skin is a coppery colour and their noses are 'aquiline' (eagle-like).

Top: An old man and child in Tibet. Both have distinctly Mongoloid features.
Right: A family of Eskimos in Canada.
Below: The map shows how the yellow-skinned peoples spread out from Mongolia.

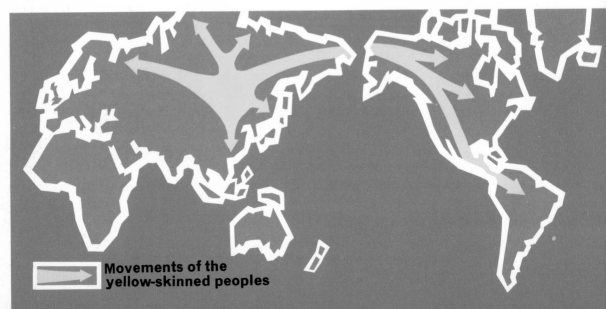

Movements of the yellow-skinned peoples

Above: A present-day Indian in South Dakota, U.S.A. In the background are the carved heads of Mt. Rushmore.

American Indians

The American (or 'Red') Indians got their name by mistake. When COLUMBUS discovered America he thought he had reached INDIA. He therefore called the natives 'Indians'.

Although the Indians had similar features, they were divided into many tribes. Their languages, customs, and lives were very different. Many hunted the BISON, from which they obtained food and clothing. This animal also provided them with covering for their tepees (tents), and even with fuel.

When the white man came to America, the life of the Indians changed greatly. The white men treated the Indians cruelly, took away their lands and killed most of the bison. In CANADA and the United States, most of the Indians who are left now live in reservations – land set apart for them. In SOUTH AMERICA, most Indians live as very poor peasants, though a few wild tribes still survive in the AMAZON jungle.

Above: A photograph of Lone Wolf, the Kiowa warrior, in about 1870. Right: An Indian chief holding a peace-pipe.

Lapps

The Lapps live in the far north of Scandinavia, mostly beyond the Arctic Circle. They are a small, dark-haired people. They speak a language similar to Finnish.

Until very recently most of them followed the great herds of REINDEER that wander about Lapland. The reindeer provided them with everything they needed – meat, milk, clothes, boots, tent-covering, transport and even tools. There are still many Lapp reindeer herdsmen. Most Lapps, however, have settled down to become farmers, fishermen or craftsmen.

Lapp men are expert bone-carvers, and the women are equally good at embroidery. Lapps often wear beautifully decorated clothes.

Left: A Lapp in traditional costume. In the background there is a reindeer.

Eskimos

There are not many more than 50,000 Eskimos living today. They live in arctic lands, such as Greenland, Labrador, Hudson Bay and Alaska. They live by HUNTING and FISHING. The climate makes any kind of farming impossible.

During the summer months Eskimos generally live in sealskin tents. In the fierce arctic winters they move to permanent stone or turf houses. Igloos – houses made from blocks of snow – are only used temporarily while the Eskimos are hunting SEALS. Eskimos travel by sleds drawn by dogs called huskies. They also use canoes called kayaks.

Eskimos originally came from ASIA. They belong to the YELLOW-SKINNED group of peoples.

An Eskimo waits with his gun for a seal to appear in a hole in the ice.

Polynesians

The Polynesians are a brown-skinned people who live on many islands in the South PACIFIC. Some scientists believe that their ancestors sailed thousands of miles in frail canoes from ASIA to their island homes. Others believe they first came from SOUTH AMERICA. Among these is Thor Heyerdahl, who built and sailed the raft *Kon-Tiki*.

The Maoris of NEW ZEALAND are of Polynesian stock. They arrived in New Zealand about six hundred years ago from some Polynesian island or islands. Today there are about 160,000 Maoris.

The Maoris were once a very warlike people. They fought fiercely against the British who colonised New Zealand. But today they are a peaceful people, often working as farmers, craftsmen, and shepherds.

Above: This old Maori woman is standing by the gateway to her village.

No one knows for certain how long Man has lived on the earth. The first men may have been walking the earth a million years ago, or perhaps much earlier.

They were different from other animals. They had better BRAINS and were more intelligent. They could think and remember, they could talk, tell each other things, and work together. They stood up straight.

Most important, they had thumbs which could touch their fingertips, and so they could hold a stick or throw a stone when they were hunting. In time they learned to make tools, light fires, and build shelters.

Man's first tools were sticks and the stones which he learned to chip into rough axes. He used these axes as weapons, and they helped him when he hunted animals. He also caught fish with spears, and fish-hooks made from thorns. Almost the only things that remain from this period, which is called the Old Stone Age, are some of the stone tools.

In the New Stone Age, people began to live together in larger groups. They learned to tame flocks and herds of domestic animals. They made picks from deer antlers and shovels from the shoulder blades of CATTLE. They also began to make pottery.

A man from the Old Stone Age, carrying a flint. He could use the flint as a weapon.

B.C.		A.D.
	Iron Age	
		1000
	Bronze Age	
		2000
	New Stone Age	
		2500
Middle Stone Age		
10,000		
	Old Stone Age	
	500,000	

	B.
3200 B.C.	Egyptians
2500 B.C.	Babylonians
	2000 B.C.
	2000 B.C.

TIME CHART
The chart on the left shows how long the Stone, Bronze, and Iron Ages lasted. The main chart shows the chief civilizations. They cover a very short period of time compared with the Stone Age.

Bronze Age

Five or six thousand years ago men first learned to mix COPPER and tin together to make bronze. This knowledge spread slowly through the world. People could now make better tools and weapons. They had helmets, shields, and ARMOUR. They could even make sharp razors and attractive ornaments.

They wove fine clothes and built ships. Their chiefs drove in chariots and lived in palaces. They built the first great cities.

Right: A beautifully decorated shield from the Iron Age.

Iron Age

In some parts of the world, the Iron Age began about four thousand years ago. Men learned to make IRON, and found that it was harder and better than bronze. In war, for instance, the man with iron weapons could defeat the man with bronze weapons.

The use of the new metal spread slowly. The Iron Age began in Europe in about 900 B.C. It began in CHINA three hundred years later, and in Britain later still. Man made great progress in this period and invented many things, including coins.

Right: This horned bronze helmet dates from about 100 B.C.

		A.D.		
520 B.C.				
538 B.C.				
	Chinese		1912 A.D. →	
Greeks	100 B.C.			
	200 B.C.	Indians of Asia	1700 A.D. →	
770 B.C. Romans	450 A.D.	Byzantine 1453		
660 B.C.	Japanese	1880 A.D →		
	325 A.D.	Mayas, Incas, Aztecs	1500 A.D.	
570 B.C.	Arabs	1260 B.C.		

Ancient Egyptians

One of the first great civilizations was in the fertile valley of the NILE. The first Pharaoh, or King of Egypt, ruled about 3200 B.C. The kingdom remained powerful for almost 3000 years. Then, the Egyptians were conquered by the Assyrians, then by the PERSIANS, and later by the Greeks led by ALEXANDER THE GREAT.

In that long period the Ancient Egyptians built up a rich empire with strong ARMIES and fleets. Using thousands of slaves, they constructed huge TEMPLES and statues, and put up pyramids to cover the tombs of their kings. The Great Pyramid was built for the Pharaoh, Cheops, in about 2700 B.C. and took nearly five million tons of stone.

The Egyptians studied the STARS and had mapped out the sky by 3000 B.C.

Top: An Egyptian bronze cat of about 600 B.C.
Right: A wooden model of an early Egyptian boat.
Below: An illustration from a scroll made of papyrus. The soul of a scribe is being weighed in the balance.

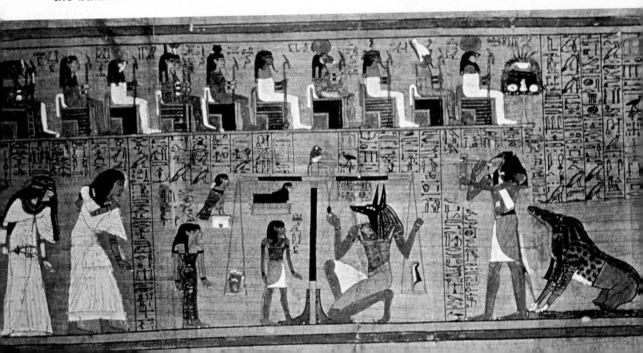

Persians

The ancient Persians were a nation of warlike people. Cyrus the Great founded their empire by conquering Babylon about 2,500 years ago. Later kings, Cambyses and Darius I, enlarged this empire by conquering EGYPT, Asia Minor (modern TURKEY), and other lands.

When the Persians tried to invade EUROPE, they were driven back by the GREEKS, and it was the Greeks under ALEXANDER who conquered the Persian Empire in 331 B.C.

After Alexander's death, his empire was divided into several parts, and Persia became less important. Later, it regained some of its earlier power before being conquered by the ARABS.

Today Persia is called IRAN.

Above: This little gold chariot was made in Ancient Persia about 500 years before Christ was born. It is drawn by four horses and is about 19 centimetres long.

Babylonians

Babylonia was the name of the land between the rivers Tigris and Euphrates. (The area is now part of Iraq.) Civilization began there at about the same date as it did in EGYPT.

Much later, the city of Babylon became the capital. The city had magnificent TEMPLES, PALACES, and bridges over the Euphrates, which flowed through the city. The Hanging Gardens, in terraces, were one of the SEVEN WONDERS OF THE WORLD.

King Hammurabi gave the Babylonians strict but fair laws. Most writing was on clay tablets. Thousands of these have been found, bearing poems, stories, and writings about science.

In 689 B.C., Babylonia became part of the Assyrian empire. 150 years later it was conquered by the PERSIANS.

A Babylonian clay tablet. The writing is in a script called cuneiform – meaning 'wedge-shaped'.

Chinese

The Chinese civilization is one of the oldest in the world. Pottery with picture-writing has been found in CHINA dating from about 4500 B.C.

Early China was made up of many small states. Then it was united under one ruler. Each ruler was thought to be sent by the gods. He was known as the Son of Heaven. In 551 B.C., the great philosopher CONFUCIUS was born. At that time, there were many writers, artists, and philosophers, and they were treated with great honour.

The Great Wall was probably built by the first emperor, Shih Huang Ti (246–210 B.C.) to keep out invaders. He also built roads and canals in order to unite the country. There were many other emperors until the revolution of A.D. 1912.

The Chinese invented many things – gunpowder, paper, PRINTING, and the ship's compass. They excelled in the making of PORCELAIN (which we call 'china' because they invented it), in water-colour painting, and in carving.

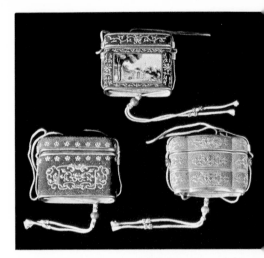

Top: A set of Chinese tinder boxes.
Above: A decorated vase.
Below: A figure of the Earth Spirit.

Below left: The Great Wall of China today.

Japanese

The ancient Japanese peoples came to their islands from the mainland of ASIA several centuries before CHRIST. All their emperors have been descended from their first ruler, Jimmu.

The Japanese learned much of their civilization from the CHINESE – arts, buildings, government, even costume. They altered it, however, to suit their own needs. They made beautiful metalwork, sculpture, and pictures.

In the ninth century, a class of warriors called *samurai* appeared in Japan. They followed a code of conduct called *bushido*, or 'knightly path'. Their power lasted until 1876, when they were forbidden to carry SWORDS.

Above: A Japanese mask.
Below: A pair of samurai swords.

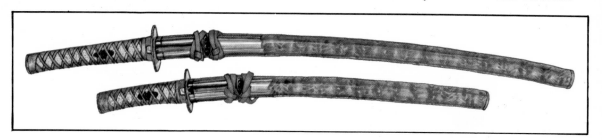

Indians of Asia

Many millions of people, with different languages, customs and religions, live in the area which in 1947 was divided into INDIA and PAKISTAN.

This region has had many rulers, outside invasions, and new mixtures in its population. Nevertheless, there have been Indian civilizations for several thousand years. The Gupta Empire, A.D. 320–500, was a golden age of HINDU culture. Much later, Moslem conquerors established the Mogul Empire, A.D. 1505–1707, which produced fine art and architecture such as the TAJ MAHAL.

Left: An Indian holy man stands in front of the Hindu temple of Minakshi in Madurai.

36

Phoenicians

The Phoenicians lived on the coast of what is now Syria and Lebanon. Their great cities were Byblos, Tyre and Sidon. They were the first great sea-traders, dealing in such goods as cedar wood, cloth, and wine. Their ships sailed all over the MEDITERRANEAN and even into the ATLANTIC.

From about 1000 B.C. onwards, they founded colonies in many lands. One colony was Carthage in North AFRICA. It later became the centre of a great empire.

Above right: A stone carving of two Phoenicians.
Right: A Phoenician dagger with its sheath.

Ancient Greeks

Greek history began in about 2000 B.C., in Crete, an island in the Aegean Sea. Then came the splendid age (1400–1000 B.C.) of the city of Mycenae on the mainland. A new tribe, the Dorians, entered the country. Many small separate 'city states' grew up in the next few centuries.

The Greeks founded trading ports throughout the MEDITERRANEAN. In time, two states, ATHENS and Sparta, became rivals for the leadership of Greece. They fought a long war which left them

Left: A small Greek statue of the goddess Aphrodite.

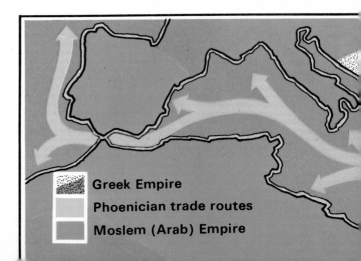

Greek Empire
Phoenician trade routes
Moslem (Arab) Empire

both weak. Then, in 338 B.C., the whole country was conquered by a northern Greek king, Philip of Macedon, father of ALEXANDER THE GREAT.

The Greeks were brilliant and original thinkers. We can still read many books they wrote, recite their poems, and act their plays. They gave us many of our ideas, including freedom and DEMOCRACY – a Greek word meaning 'government by the people'. The first OLYMPIC GAMES were held by the Greeks.

Right: A Greek mosaic of a horse and rider.

Arabs

The Arabs were a little-known desert people until they found a great leader in MOHAMMED (about A.D. 570–632). He gave them a new religion (ISLAM), and just before his death he launched them on a 'holy war' against non-believers.

The Arabs, who were also called Saracens, were fine horsemen and soldiers. In the next hundred years, their armies conquered much of western ASIA, North AFRICA, SPAIN, and Portugal. But they were driven back in FRANCE. They created a rich civilization, especially in Baghdad, Sicily, and Spain, with beautiful PALACES, gardens, and fountains. For many years they led the world in science and medical skill.

Above: An Arab of today in traditional dress.
Below: An Arab astrolabe (star-dial).

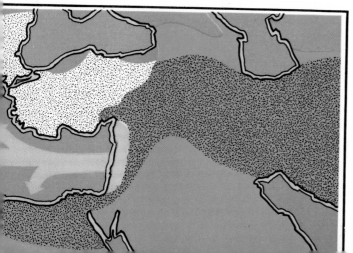

38

Ancient Romans

ROME was founded in about 750 B.C. by one of the Latin tribes of central ITALY. Until 510 B.C. the Romans had kings. Then they formed a REPUBLIC. Two consuls were elected to govern for one year, instead of the kings. They were helped by a senate of elder citizens.

The Romans had many enemies, but they were a tough people. They invented a fighting unit – the legion – so well trained that few could stand against it. The Romans conquered all Italy. They went on to take over EUROPE west of the Rhine and Danube, along with North AFRICA and Western ASIA to make a great empire.

In time, the consuls could no longer control this huge empire. A strong man was needed to rule for life. JULIUS CAESAR (murdered 44 B.C.) was the first of these men, but his great-nephew, Augustus, became the first emperor.

Right: An Ancient Roman centurion. A centurion was an army officer in charge of a hundred men.

The empire lasted about 500 years. It was overthrown by barbarian invaders between A.D. 300 and 400. Until then, despite disasters and CIVIL WARS, it mostly gave its subjects peace and good government. Famous emperors included Claudius, who brought Britain under Roman rule, the soldiers Trajan and Hadrian, and Constantine the Great.

The Romans copied many of their ideas from the GREEKS. They were, however, a more practical people than the Greeks. They were better at building straight roads, bridges and arched AQUEDUCTS to carry clean water to their cities. Our ideas of justice and orderly government came from the Romans. Their language was Latin. We still read their literature today.

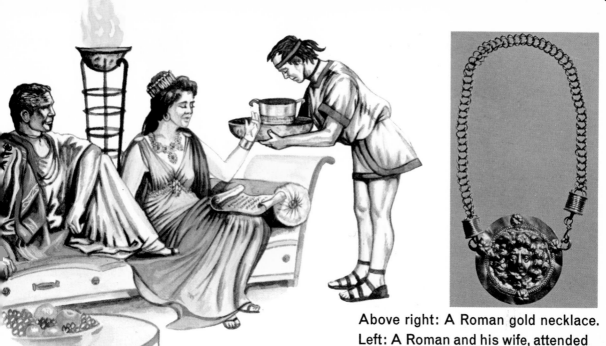

Above right: A Roman gold necklace.
Left: A Roman and his wife, attended
by a slave.

Byzantine Empire

Byzantium (now called ISTANBUL) was an ancient
Greek city. When the Roman Empire became so
big that it had to be divided, Byzantium became
the capital of the Eastern Empire. It was known
as Constantinople. When the Western Empire
fell, the Eastern half continued for a thousand
years, until the Turks conquered it in A.D. 1453.

The Byzantine emperors kept a magnificent
court, where visitors were dazzled by the rich
robes and complicated ceremonies. Church
robes are still copied from Byzantine styles.
Greek, not Latin, was spoken.

Byzantium has left us beautiful churches and
MOSAICS (pictures made with small pieces of
stone).

Right: A mosaic (a picture made up of hundreds
of tiny coloured stones) of the Byzantine Empress
Theodora. She is surrounded by ladies of the
court.

Anglo-Saxons

The Angles, Saxons, and Jutes were tribes of ancient GERMANY. They used to raid Britain during the Roman occupation. Then, from A.D. 449, they began to make Britain their home, slowly driving the Celtic Britons westwards into Wales and Cornwall. This slow conquest was completed in A.D. 825. In this year England was united for a time when King Egbert became master of all the country except for the far north.

The Anglo-Saxons were farmers and country-dwellers. Most modern English villages have grown from their early settlements. At first the Anglo-Saxons worshipped pagan gods. Then St Augustine arrived from ROME in A.D. 597 and soon all Anglo-Saxons had become Christians.

Above: The Great Buckle, from the Sutton Hoo burial ship.
Below: Anglo-Saxons ploughing.

Vikings

The Vikings were known also as Northmen, Norsemen, or Danes. Most of them were farmers. They were a fierce, warlike people.

The Vikings were overcrowded in their bleak northern lands, and so they sailed in their long-ships to Iceland, Greenland, and even NORTH AMERICA. From A.D. 787 they began invading Britain, Ireland, and FRANCE, and seized large

A carving from the prow (or front) of a Viking ship.

areas. They raided as far south as SPAIN and ITALY.

The Vikings were not mere pirates. They were also traders. They founded Dublin, Nottingham and many other towns. Their adventures are told in long stories called sagas.

A Viking longship. The sail was used when the wind was blowing in the right direction. Otherwise oars were used. The small picture shows the rowers seated on wooden boxes, which also contained their belongings.

Normans

The French king allowed some Northmen (or VIKINGS) to settle in northern FRANCE in A.D. 911. They were known as Normans. They became Christians, learned civilized ways, and in time spoke Norman French, but they kept the warlike and adventurous spirit of the Vikings.

In 1066 their duke, WILLIAM THE CONQUEROR, claimed the crown of England and won it at the Battle of Hastings. At the same time, other Normans seized southern ITALY and Sicily. Both there and in England they established strong governments. Some of their fine stone CATHEDRALS and CASTLES can still be seen.

The Bayeux Tapestry is a piece of embroidery. It shows events in the Norman Conquest of England.

Mayas

The Mayas were an ancient AMERICAN INDIAN people living in Yucatan, on the south-eastern borders of MEXICO. Their great period was A.D. 300–900, but their civilization revived later. It lasted until the Spaniards came in about A.D. 1500.

They were talented architects and artists. Many of their stepped pyramids and the TEMPLES where they made sacrifices to their gods are still standing. Their priests studied the stars and mathematics. They worked out an accurate calendar and reckoned time from 3113 B.C.

Aztecs

The Aztecs were a wandering AMERICAN INDIAN people who moved southwards from what is now the U.S.A. They settled in MEXICO about A.D. 1200, where they built their capital Tenochtitlan in A.D. 1325.

They made fine clothes, carvings, and coloured pottery. They also built pyramids, and sacrificed prisoners to the God of War. Their last emperor, Montezuma, was defeated by the Spaniards in A.D. 1520.

A stepped Mayan temple. The three figures on the right are priests. As children, their heads were tightly bound up. This made their heads very long.

Incas

The Incas were an AMERICAN INDIAN tribe. They ruled an empire of subject peoples extending over Peru, Ecuador, and the north of Chile. They came from the south about A.D. 1100 and made their capital at Cuzco, high in the Andes. Their important buildings were covered with sheets of gold. The ruler of the empire was called the 'Unique Inca', and was treated like a god.

The Incas built bridges, paved roads, and made AQUEDUCTS. They could move ten-ton blocks of stone. They had no system of writing, however, and had not thought of the wheel. The Spanish general, Pizarro, conquered them in A.D. 1533.

From the earliest times, men have held religious beliefs. Religions arise from the idea that forces more powerful than man control him and the universe. Primitive man worshipped objects, such as rivers and mountains, or the sun or moon. Later peoples, such as the EGYPTIANS and the GREEKS and ROMANS, believed in a number of gods. Sometimes they made models, or images, of their gods, and sometimes worshipped the images themselves.

Many religions today teach that there is only one God. Jews and Christians share this belief. The followers of most of the main religions also believe in some kind of life after death. In addition, many religions tell their followers how they should behave on earth. A sect is a group of members of one religion, who have certain beliefs of their own. Most of the main religions are divided up into a number of sects.

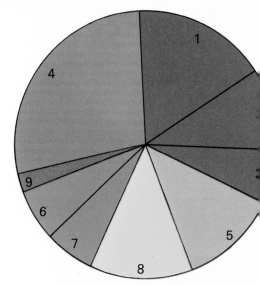

Above: The diagram shows the population of the world by religions. Below: The official religions of the world. Today many people do not follow a religion.

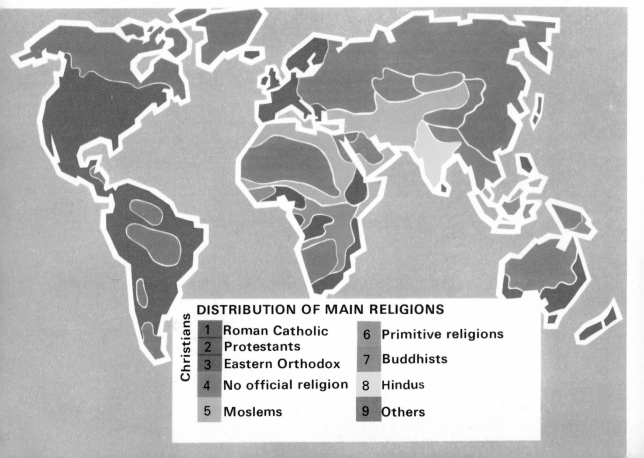

DISTRIBUTION OF MAIN RELIGIONS

Christians

1	Roman Catholic	6	Primitive religions
2	Protestants	7	Buddhists
3	Eastern Orthodox	8	Hindus
4	No official religion	9	Others
5	Moslems		

Hindus

Hinduism is INDIA's main religion. Its oldest scriptures, the Veda hymns, are thousands of years old. Hindus worship God in many different forms. The three most important forms are Brahma the Creator, Vishnu the Preserver, and Shiva the Destroyer.

Hindus believe that they are born again many times. They are born in a higher or lower state depending on the life they have led. They believe that they can live a series of better and better lives until they attain the state of *moksha*. At this point they are freed from the need to be born again. Not all Hindus have exactly the same customs and beliefs.

Right: A carnival horse at a Hindu festival in Madras, India. Festivals like this one are part of India's colourful tradition.

Buddhists

Siddartha Gautama, founder of Buddhism, was a HINDU prince, born about 550 B.C. He is called the Buddha, or 'the enlightened one'. He thought deeply about pain and the best way to live in the world. He spent most of his life teaching people to follow the law of *Karma*, which meant giving up earthly desires to reach the perfect peace of *Nirvana*. In order to do this a man must follow the Noble Eightfold Way, which lays down rules for correct behaviour.

Buddhists believe that creatures are born many times. They also consider it wrong to kill. Buddhist teachings were not written down until about 100 B.C. Today about one-fifth of the human race follow Buddhism. Most Buddhists live in CHINA, JAPAN, and other parts of ASIA.

The Great Buddha at Kamakura in Japan.
This huge statue was made in the 13th century.

Islam

Islam means 'to submit'. It is the religion of the Moslems who live in the ARAB countries, PAKISTAN, and other parts of ASIA. They have one God, Allah, and their sacred book is the Koran.

Like Jews and Christians, Moslems believe in the Old Testament prophets, or teachers, such as Moses. They say also that JESUS was a great prophet but not the Son of God. They think that the greatest prophet of all was MOHAMMED, the founder of Islam, an Arab who died in A.D. 632.

Right: The Kaaba is an important Moslem shrine in Mecca. Inside, it is empty. The band around the black covering contains writings in gold.

Judaism

Judaism is the religion of the Jews. Jewish teaching is based on the books of the Old Testament, and a collection of writings called the Talmud. Jews believe that, through their teacher Moses, God gave them the Ten Commandments, and other rules for living.

Like Christians, Jews believe in one God. Strict Jews keep Saturday as their Sabbath, or day of rest. They must not marry non-Jews. They may not eat pork. Their ministers are called rabbis, and their services are held in synagogues. Today Jewish people live all over the world, as well as in ISRAEL.

Above: A Jewish synagogue. The Star of David appears on the gate. Left: The Western (or Wailing) Wall in Jerusalem is an ancient Jewish relic.

Christianity

Christianity is the faith of those who believe that JESUS, a young Jewish teacher, was in fact the Son of God sent on earth to show men how to live. Thousands flocked to hear Jesus preach, but He also had powerful enemies. He was put to death in about A.D. 30, but His disciples, or followers, said that He had risen again and that people had seen Him. They went on spreading the Gospel or 'good news' that God was the loving Father of all and that there was a better life after death.

Several wrote down all they remembered about Jesus. These writings are called the Gospels of Matthew, Mark, Luke, and John. They form the beginning of the New Testament. Joined with the Old Testament, the sacred writings of JUDAISM, it forms the Bible.

Jesus was also called Christ, a Greek word meaning 'the anointed one'. His followers came to be called Christians. Soon they spread all over the Roman Empire. In A.D. 380, Emperor Constantine made Christianity the official religion.

Top: A painting of the dead Christ by Bellini.
Left: Christ and His mother, as imagined by an Australian aborigine.
Below: The Altar of Golgotha, in Jerusalem.

48

Roman Catholics

Early Christians belonged to one 'catholic' (world-wide) church, but in time they divided into the Roman Catholic and the EASTERN CHURCH. The head of the Roman Catholics is the Pope, the bishop of ROME, but there are other bishops and priests in most parts of the world. These bishops and priests may not marry.

Catholics (laymen) must keep the Church's rules, confessing their sins and going to the service called Mass each Sunday. They believe that Christ's Mother, the Virgin Mary, and the Saints can help them when they pray to God.

Right: The Pope is the head of the Roman Catholic Church. Here, Pope Paul VI kneels in prayer, during a visit to the Holy Land.

Protestants

After the Middle Ages, some Christians thought that the ROMAN CATHOLIC faith was no longer true to Christ's teaching. A German monk, MARTIN LUTHER, led their protest in 1517. His followers (the PROTESTANTS) broke away and formed their own churches. They refused to obey the Pope. They also changed the services, and had married men as ministers.

Protestant churches include the Church of England, the Church of Scotland, and the Lutheran Churches of NORWAY, DENMARK, SWEDEN, and GERMANY itself. A later development was the Protestant Episcopal Church of the United States.

Left: Martin Luther was one of the early leaders of the Protestant movement. He did not agree with all the teachings of the Catholic Church. He made a list of his beliefs, and nailed it to the door of a church in Wittenberg.

Methodists

The first Methodists were a group of students from Oxford University led by JOHN WESLEY (1703–1791) and his brother Charles. They decided to live 'methodically' and met often for religious study and prayer. They thought that the Church of England was not following its own rules. They did not want to leave it but in time they were forced out. They then formed a church of their own. At first, they held their prayer meetings out of doors.

Today there are several different kinds of Methodists spread over the world. Methodist Churches are organised in groups called circuits. A group of circuits forms a district. The head of a district is called a chairman, or, in the U.S.A., a bishop.

Right: Barratts Chapel, in Delaware, U.S.A. It is known as the 'Cradle of Methodism' in America.

Eastern Church

The Eastern (or Orthodox) Church began after the capital of the Roman Empire had been moved to Constantinople, now ISTANBUL. Later, it refused to accept the Pope as the head of the Christian Church. In 1054 it separated from the Western (ROMAN CATHOLIC) Church.

The Eastern Church spread to a number of countries, mainly GREECE and Russia. The Russian Church has survived attempts to suppress it by the Communist Party, which does not approve of religion.

The archbishops of the Eastern Church are known as patriarchs or metropolitans. Saints are considered to be very important. They are often represented by small images called icons.

A typical Greek Orthodox Church in Thessalonica.

Quakers

'Quakers' was the name given to the Society of Friends because they sometimes trembled with excitement at their meetings in the early days. The Society was founded by George Fox in 1652, spread quickly through Britain, and by 1656 had its first members in NORTH AMERICA. One Quaker, William Penn, founded Pennsylvania, U.S.A.

Quakers believe in a simple, strict, sincere way of life, based on the goodness of every man. They worship God in quiet meetings. They will not fight as soldiers but will risk their lives to help the wounded.

Right: George Fox, who founded the Society of Friends in 1652. He was put in prison for his beliefs on many occasions. He lived for a time in America.

Mormons

The official name of the Mormon Church is the Church of Jesus Christ of the Latter-Day Saints. Joseph Smith claimed he had seen a vision of God and had been given a new gospel, the Book of Mormon. He founded the Church in 1830.

The Mormons settled first in Missouri, and then in Illinois. In both places there were conflicts with their neighbours, and Joseph Smith was killed.

In 1847, Brigham Young, their second leader, led them to what is now Utah, where they founded Salt Lake City. At first, the men often had several wives, but later Mormons gave up this practice, as it was against U.S. law. Today they are a wealthy church. Mormons have always sent missionaries to other countries.

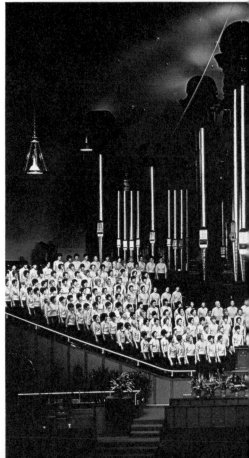

The choir of the Mormon Tabernacle, in Salt Lake City, Utah. The choir is famous all over the world.

Presbyterians

These Christians, who follow the teachings of the reformer, John CALVIN (1509–1564), believe that the Church should be directed by 'Elders' (Senior Church Members), not bishops. 'Presbyter' is the Greek word for 'Elder' and so they are called Presbyterians in some parts of the world. Another name which became common in England is 'Congregationalists', since they believe that each congregation, with its elders and members, should be self-governing. There are many Presbyterians in Britain, the NETHERLANDS, the U.S.A. and SOUTH AFRICA.

In other parts of the world the followers of Calvin are known as Calvinists; for example, the Dutch Reformed Churches of South Africa. There are three such Churches: Nederduitse Gereformeerde Kerk, the Gereformeerde Kerk, and the Nederduitsch Hervormde Kerk van Afrika. The French and Swiss Reformed Churches are also Calvinists.

Above left: The Swiss reformer John Calvin.

Christian Scientists

Christian Science was founded by Mary Baker Eddy in America in 1879. She wrote a book called *Science and Health, with Key to the Scriptures.* She taught that sickness exists only in one's mind, and can be cured by correct thoughts.

Jehovah's Witnesses

Jehovah (or 'Yahweh') was the ancient Jewish name for God. 'Jehovah's Witnesses' is the name given, since 1931, to the Watch Tower Bible and Tract Society. This group was founded in the United States in 1872 by Charles Taze Russell. Its members believe that the end of the world is near and that Christ will return to earth.

The stories and ideas of a group of peoples, which are handed down from parents to children, are called folklore. Early religions were closely connected with folklore. The ANCIENT GREEKS told stories, not only about gods, but about the heroes who were nearly as powerful as the gods.

Before people understood the scientific reasons for things happening, they explained them by magical or superstitious ideas. People thought that natural events like tides and seasons were caused by the gods. It was therefore important not to make the gods angry. Even today we have a number of SUPERSTITIONS.

Many old customs survive long after their original purpose has disappeared. Holly and mistletoe were used in religious ceremonies long before CHRISTIANITY.

The Greeks and Romans worshipped a number of gods and goddesses. They believed that the gods lived on the top of Mount Olympus. The king of the gods was called Zeus (1). The Romans called him Jupiter. The queen was called Hera (Juno to the Romans). Other gods included Apollo (3), the sun-god; Artemis (2) (Diana), goddess of the moon and hunting; Aphrodite (Venus), goddess of love; Ares (Mars), god of war; Poseidon (5) (Neptune), god of the sea; Dionysus (4) (Bacchus) was god of wine and drama; Hermes (6) (Mercury) was the messenger of the gods.

Myths

Myths are the stories that have grown up among various peoples to explain things they could not fully understand. The GREEKS, for example, said the SUN was really a young god, Apollo, driving a golden chariot across the sky. Myths were passed down by word of mouth before there were any books. Each people has its own group of myths, but some groups of myths have been influenced by others.

Different peoples have had different stories to explain similar things. Some held that the world was supported by the giant Atlas. Others believed that it rested on four elephants riding on the back of a swimming turtle.

Left: A painting of a mythical subject – the Birth of the Milky Way, by Tintoretto.

Norse Gods

Before they became Christians, the ANGLO-SAXONS and other German tribes believed in many gods. The king of the gods was Odin, or Woden, the All-Father, the Lord of Hosts. He lived in Asgard (heaven) and had a hall, Valhalla, where dead heroes led a life of fighting and feasting.

Odin's wife was named Frigg, but a much more important goddess was Freya, who drove a chariot drawn by cats. Odin's sons were the mighty thunder god Thor, and the gentle Balder, who was killed by the evil god, Loki. Wednesday is named after Woden, Thursday after Thor, and Friday after Freya.

Below left: Three of the most important Norse gods. Odin is on the left, and Thor is in the centre. Balder stands on the right. Thor was believed to cause thunder with blows from his hammer.

Legends

Like MYTHS, legends are old stories. But most legends are based on something that actually happened. Stories about King Arthur and Robin Hood are legends, even though there probably *was* a man like King Arthur, and perhaps even one like Robin Hood. There was a real city of Troy, though the tale told in the *Iliad* is only legend. So are the oldest stories about ROME. It is often difficult to distinguish the historical part of legends from the part that has been made up.

The Norsemen retold their early adventures in sagas that are mostly legend, and the Russians had legends of Prince Igor and Sadko the Minstrel. The French legend of Roland and his magic war-horn is almost certainly based on an actual fight in the mountains.

The Irish have legends of Cuchullin and the Red Branch Knights, the Scots tell of the Fairy Flag of Dunvegan Castle, the Welsh of Princess Branwen. One could go round the world listing legends from those of Rama in INDIA to the adventures of the U.S. folk hero, Paul Bunyan.

Above: William Tell, the hero of many legends, lived in Switzerland. Below: The legend of Saint George and the dragon, painted by Uccello.

Mythical Beasts

The ANCIENT EGYPTIANS had a number of gods which were part man and part animals. The hawk-headed god Horus was one of these. Another strange creature was the Sphinx, which was a winged lion with a woman's head.

The ANCIENT GREEKS had a number of LEGENDS connected with monsters. In one story, King Minos kept a monster called a minotaur in a labyrinth, or maze. It was eventually killed by Theseus, who found his way back by following a thread he had unwound through the paths of the labyrinth. Another monster often mentioned in Greek MYTHS was the centaur. It was portrayed as half man and half horse.

The chimera was an even stranger creature. It breathed fire, and devastated the countryside. It was killed by Bellerophon, riding on the back of the winged horse Pegasus.

Above: In Greek legend, the minotaur was a fierce monster. It had the body of a man, but the head of a bull. It lived on human sacrifices.

The chimera was a mythical beast, part lion, part goat, part dragon.

Superstitions

Not walking under ladders, not spilling salt, 'unlucky 13' – these are just a few of many superstitions.

Superstitions are old ideas that are left over from the days of magical beliefs. In those days people knew nothing of science and often did not understand the real reasons why certain things happened. Most people do not seriously believe in superstitions, but they remain as habits.

Witches

Until about three hundred years ago, most people believed in witches. Some still do. Witches were people who claimed that they could help or harm other people with MAGIC charms or spells.

We normally think of witches as women, but there were men witches as well. Men witches used to be called wizards, or witch-doctors in AFRICA (where they are still occasionally found).

Top left: Some of the things that are connected with superstitions. In some parts of the world black cats are thought to be unlucky. In other countries they are considered lucky.

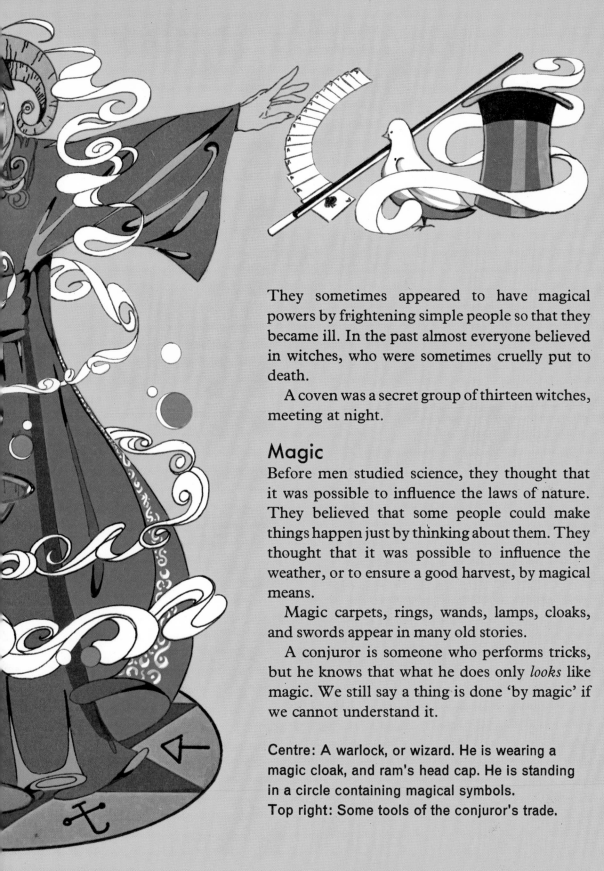

They sometimes appeared to have magical powers by frightening simple people so that they became ill. In the past almost everyone believed in witches, who were sometimes cruelly put to death.

A coven was a secret group of thirteen witches, meeting at night.

Magic

Before men studied science, they thought that it was possible to influence the laws of nature. They believed that some people could make things happen just by thinking about them. They thought that it was possible to influence the weather, or to ensure a good harvest, by magical means.

Magic carpets, rings, wands, lamps, cloaks, and swords appear in many old stories.

A conjuror is someone who performs tricks, but he knows that what he does only *looks* like magic. We still say a thing is done 'by magic' if we cannot understand it.

Centre: A warlock, or wizard. He is wearing a magic cloak, and ram's head cap. He is standing in a circle containing magical symbols.
Top right: Some tools of the conjuror's trade.

Agriculture

Forestry

Scientific Research

Exploration

Medicine

The people who control the running of a country are usually called its government.

The government makes the laws and organises many things which people cannot do separately for themselves. It maintains an ARMY and a POLICE force, and builds ROADS. In some countries the government also builds many of the houses, owns the RAILWAYS, runs the postal services, and provides schools and hospitals.

The government needs money to pay for these things and for many other purposes, such as old age pensions and sickness benefit. It collects the money it needs from the people in TAXES.

In some countries, governments spend a lot of money on space programmes, such as the Apollo launches (below).

Democracy

Democracy is a Greek word and means 'government by the people'. In a true democracy, everyone has a say in the way the country is run.

This form of government developed in ANCIENT GREECE when each state was so small that every man could go to a meeting and vote. Now that states have millions of citizens, people have to choose a few men to speak and vote for them. Different countries choose these men in different ways.

Monarchy

Monarchy means a system of government by one ruler for his lifetime. A monarch is usually a king or queen, emperor or empress. He or she comes to power as the child or nearest relative of the monarch before.

Modern monarchs, like the Queen of England and the King of NORWAY, usually leave the running of the government to their ministers, who have been elected to their job. But the monarch still acts as the head of the nation.

The number of countries that still have a monarchy is becoming smaller. Other countries that still have a king, queen, or emperor include BELGIUM, DENMARK, SWEDEN, the NETHERLANDS, IRAN, and JAPAN.

Communism

Communism is the theory that all property should be owned by the state. In return the state should give everyone everything he or she needs. This theory was put forward by KARL MARX, and is also sometimes called Marxism. CHINA, the Soviet Union, and several other countries are trying to work towards this situation. Many people object to Communism because they do not want total control by the state.

Above: King Baudouin and Queen Fabiola of the Belgians.
Below: Edward VII became King of England in 1901.

Republic

A republic is a government where there is no king. Nowadays the leader is usually called a PRESIDENT. Officials in a republic are voted into office by the people of the country.

The ANCIENT ROMANS had a republic from 510 to 31 B.C. Later on, EUROPE was mainly ruled by emperors and kings, until republics were founded again by the Swiss, the Italians, and the Dutch. England was a republic for a time under OLIVER CROMWELL. The U.S.A. became the first of the great modern republics.

Right: This painting shows the U.S. Congress voting for Independence from Britain. From being a colony, the United States became a republic.

Revolutions

Revolutions happen when people are not satisfied with the way their country is run. After a revolution a country has new rulers (the word *revolution* means 'to turn around'). Russia had two revolutions in 1917.

Robespierre (3) was a leader in the French Revolution. He executed many opponents by guillotine (4). The Russian Revolution of 1905 (1) failed, but the Bolsheviks (7) under Lenin (2) were successful in 1917. In 1956 the Russians crushed a revolution (6) in Hungary. 'Che' Guevara (5) was a revolutionary in South America.

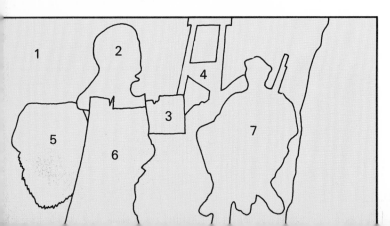

The United States was founded as the result of the Revolution of 1776. As well as the Russian Communist Revolution of 1917, other important revolutions are: the French Revolutions of 1789, 1830, and 1848, and the two Chinese Revolutions of 1911 and 1949.

Dictatorship

A dictator is a man who takes over the government of a country, often by force, after a REVOLUTION. Often, he breaks the law of that country and makes new laws to suit himself, without letting people vote. Modern dictators have included HITLER (GERMANY), Mussolini (ITALY), and STALIN (Russia).

Above: Benito Mussolini was dictator of Italy from 1922, until he was executed in 1945.

United Nations

The United Nations came into existence in 1945. It began as an association of 50 countries, but many more joined later. Its first aim is to stop future wars by giving governments a chance to meet and settle their disputes peacefully.

It also tries to get countries to work together and help each other. The richer nations give or lend money to the poorer ones. When there is a flood, famine, or an EARTHQUAKE, the other countries send food, tents, DOCTORS, and medicines. When certain illnesses break out, governments help each other so that the infection does not spread.

Meetings are held at the headquarters in NEW YORK, where the Secretary General works with his staff. Each nation votes in the General Assembly, but only 15 are chosen for the Security Council, which has more power.

Above: The United Nations symbol. Below: A meeting of the Security Council. Fifteen countries are represented on the Council. The U.S.A., Great Britain, France, Russia, and China are always on it. Other countries are on it in turn.

Commonwealth

The Commonwealth is the name now given to the old British Empire. All but the very smallest Commonwealth countries (like the little islands of the PACIFIC OCEAN) now have their own governments and are not governed by Britain. But many of these countries, such as CANADA, regard the Queen as their queen. Even those which have become REPUBLICS, like INDIA, remain members of the Commonwealth and accept her as its head. The prime ministers of the Commonwealth countries meet from time to time.

Commonwealth once meant government without a MONARCHY. After the execution of King Charles I of England, the rule of OLIVER CROMWELL was known as the Commonwealth.

Below: Commonwealth leaders with Her Majesty Queen Elizabeth II during a meeting in London.

COUNTRIES OF THE COMMONWEALTH

Australia	Malta
Bangladesh	Mauritius
Barbados	Nauru
Botswana	New Zealand
Canada	Nigeria
Cyprus	Sierra Leone
Fiji	Singapore
The Gambia	Sri Lanka
Ghana	Swaziland
Guyana	Tanzania
India	Tonga
Jamaica	Trinidad and Tobago
Kenya	Uganda
Lesotho	United Kingdom
Malawi	Western Samoa
Malaysia	Zambia

Elections

Elections are held so that citizens can choose people to run their government. Countries have different systems. Usually, there is a secret ballot. Nobody knows how anyone else votes.

The U.S.A. has an election for PRESIDENT every four years. In Britain, PARLIAMENT must hold a General Election at least every five years. The election may come sooner if it seems necessary to choose a new parliament. In some countries elections are not free, because the government allows votes for only one person or candidate.

Right: The election of the U.S. Democratic Party presidential candidate in 1972.
Centre right: The election of candidates for the Electoral College in New Guinea.
Below: A British election poster.

Political Parties

People with the same ideas on how to run the government often join a political party. They hold meetings, give out leaflets, and try in every way to get their leaders chosen to rule the country. They have to collect a lot of money to pay for these things.

In a free country, any group of people can form a party. In the U.S.A., there are two big parties, the Democrats and the Republicans. In Britain the main parties are the Conservatives (Tories) and the Labour Party, or Socialists.

Some countries have even more parties. Social Democrat parties are much the same as the Labour Party in Britain. Often two or more parties may have to join together to form a government. But in the U.S.S.R., CHINA, and other countries where the Communist Party is in power, no other parties are allowed. Anyone trying to form one may be put in PRISON.

WHEN IT COMES DOWN TO IT-AREN'T LABOUR'S IDEALS YOURS AS WELL?

Common Market

The Common Market is the simple name for the European Economic Community (E.E.C.). It began in 1957 when the Treaty of Rome was signed by six nations: FRANCE, GERMANY, ITALY, BELGIUM, THE NETHERLANDS, and LUXEMBOURG. They agreed to work together in trading and many other things as if they were one country.

Britain at first belonged to the European Free Trade Association (EFTA). In 1973, with DENMARK and the Republic of IRELAND, Britain joined the Common Market. In June 1975, the British people voted to remain in the E.E.C.

Above: The headquarters of the Common Market in Brussels.

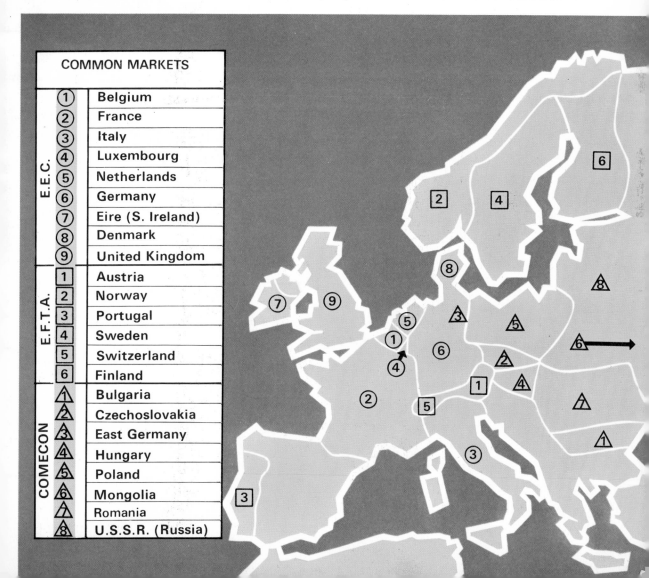

COMMON MARKETS		
E.E.C.	①	Belgium
	②	France
	③	Italy
	④	Luxembourg
	⑤	Netherlands
	⑥	Germany
	⑦	Eire (S. Ireland)
	⑧	Denmark
	⑨	United Kingdom
E.F.T.A.	1	Austria
	2	Norway
	3	Portugal
	4	Sweden
	5	Switzerland
	6	Finland
COMECON	△1	Bulgaria
	△2	Czechoslovakia
	△3	East Germany
	△4	Hungary
	△5	Poland
	△6	Mongolia
	△7	Romania
	△8	U.S.S.R. (Russia)

Parliament

A parliament is the place where laws are made, TAXES are fixed, and all matters of government are discussed.

The British Parliament meets at Westminster, in LONDON, and is often called 'the mother of parliaments' because it is so old and has been

A plan of the Debating Chamber of the British House of Commons. The Speaker has to try to keep order.

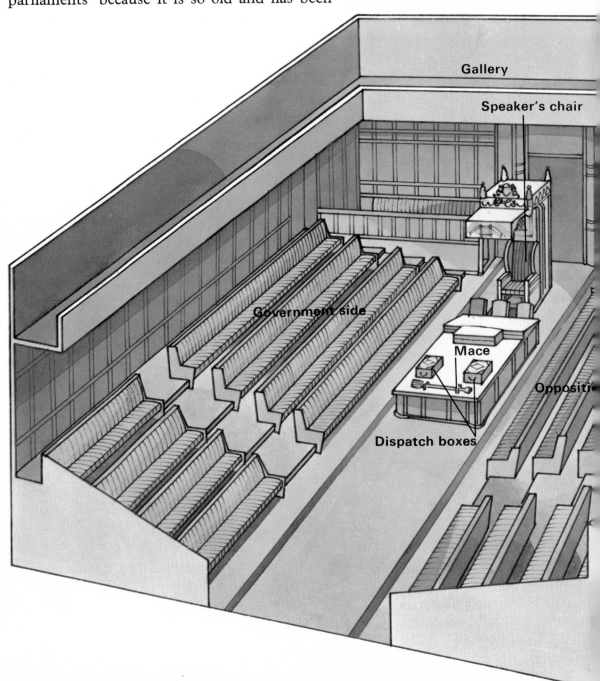

Gallery

Speaker's chair

Government side

Mace

Opposition

Dispatch boxes

Speaker

copied in so many other countries. Often these other countries use a different name, such as CONGRESS or National Assembly, but the basic idea is the same. When the people of a country are free to elect the government they want, the system is called 'parliamentary DEMOCRACY'.

The British Parliament consists of three parts: the Queen, the House of Lords and the House of Commons. Laws have to be passed in both Houses and signed by the Queen.

The House of Commons has about 630 M.P.s (Members of Parliament), each chosen by voters in one area or division. Those who support the Government sit on one side of the House. The others face them. One M.P. is made Speaker, or chairman, to keep order.

A new law begins as a Bill. When it has been debated (talked over) in both Houses and agreed, the Queen also gives it her assent (approval) and it becomes an Act (is made law).

Prime Minister

A Prime Minister is the head of the governing party. Sometimes, as in FRANCE, the Prime Minister has less power than the PRESIDENT. In Britain he has more power than anyone else. He is usually the leader of the party in power.

The Queen asks him to 'form a government'. He chooses other ministers to help him. He is given a house and office at 10 Downing Street in LONDON near the House of Commons and a quieter country home at Chequers. When he cannot get PARLIAMENT to vote as he wishes, he must either resign or hold an ELECTION.

Left: William Pitt the Younger. At the age of twenty-four he became Britain's youngest-ever Prime Minister.

Congress

Congress is the body which makes laws for the United States. Like the British PARLIAMENT, it meets in two parts, the SENATE and the HOUSE OF REPRESENTATIVES. They use the north and south wings of the great Capitol building in WASHINGTON, D.C.

Congress is bound by the rules, or Constitution, of the United States and needs a two-to-one vote to alter those rules. The PRESIDENT can put a ban or veto on what Congress decides, unless there is a two-thirds majority against him.

Senate

The first senate was in ancient ROME. Now it is the name given in many countries to the 'upper house' of the body making their laws. The United States Senate is part of CONGRESS. It has 100 members. Two senators are elected from each of the 50 states and serve for six years each. But one third of the senators retire every two years. In this way, the people can vote to change their senate by degrees, but not all at once.

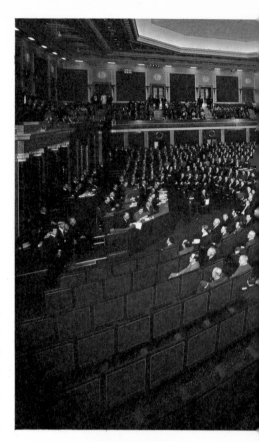

President

In a REPUBLIC, the president is head of the state and is treated almost like a king. He is often elected for life but sometimes for a fixed term –

PRESIDENTS OF THE UNITED STATES
(1) George Washington. (2) Thomas Jefferson.
(3) Andrew Jackson. (4) Abraham Lincoln.
(5) John F. Kennedy.

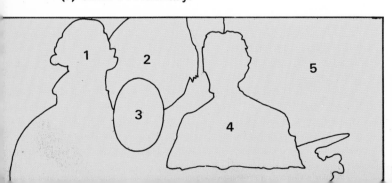

The United States House of Representatives.

four years in the United States unless the people vote for him again. He cannot now serve more than two terms.

Like modern kings, some presidents have little real power – for example, in ITALY and INDIA the government is actually run by the PRIME MINISTER. In many other republics, for example the ones in SOUTH AMERICA, the president is the most important man in the country.

House of Representatives

The House of Representatives is much bigger than the SENATE. It is also part of the United States CONGRESS. It has 435 members. Each state sends its two senators, whether it has a large population or a small one. However, the number of its Representatives depends on the number of voters. Unlike senators, they have to stand again for ELECTION every two years.

Civil Service

Civil servants are men and women who work in the different departments, or agencies, of a government. These departments include defence, health, education, and housing. Civil servants carry out the policies of the government, even if they do not agree with them. Today many countries have a large civil service, which employs thousands of people. Senior civil servants may be highly paid, expert officials.

In the United States, civil servants used to be changed when a new PRESIDENT was elected. This practice was called the 'spoils system'. In 1883 an act was passed which introduced the 'merit system'. The new system meant that people could only get into certain grades in the civil service by passing an examination. Most countries now use the merit system.

In Britain, the head of a department is called a minister. He is a member of the government. The most important ministers have places in the cabinet, and advise the PRIME MINISTER. Unlike permanent civil servants, the minister is usually replaced when there is a change of government.

Above: The Chancellor of the Exchequer is a senior minister in the British cabinet.
Below: The organization of a civil service department.

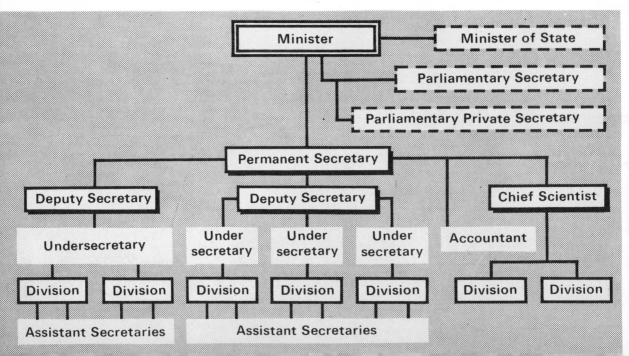

Ambassador

An ambassador represents his country in a foreign land. He explains to the rulers of that country what his own government is doing or thinking about certain matters. He also looks after his country's affairs and interests in the country to which he is sent.

He tries to settle arguments between the two countries and to help them understand each other better. He has a big official house called an embassy, and often has a large staff of officials who are called diplomats.

Left: An ambassador's staff work in an embassy. This is the United States Embassy in Grosvenor Square, London.

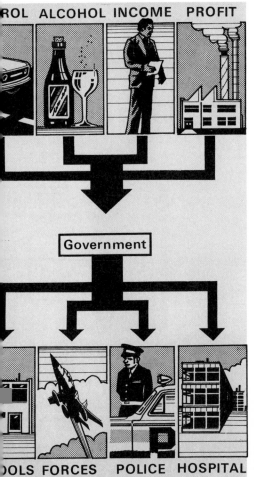

Taxes

Taxes are the money people have to give their government to pay for ARMIES, HEALTH SERVICES, schools, pensions, and many other things. People pay taxes both directly, out of their pay, and indirectly, every time they buy certain things.

The largest direct tax is Income Tax, which is based on how much money a person gets in a year. People pay indirect taxes on such goods as beer, tobacco, and cars.

Companies have to pay tax on their profits. In some countries, the money people leave when they die is also heavily taxed.

Taxes change from time to time, and each country has its own system. In Britain there is a system of local taxes called rates. In the United States there are separate state and city taxes.

Below left: All the money spent by a government has to be collected as taxes. The diagram shows where some of the money comes from. It also shows where most of the money is spent.

Laws are the rules people need to agree upon if they are to live in peace together. From the earliest times, and in the most savage tribes, laws have been made to say what men may do and what they may not. People cannot obey the law, however, unless they know what it is. So one of the first marks of a civilized people is to have its laws clearly written down and known by everyone.

Nearly four thousand years ago, King Hammurabi gave a code of laws to the BABYLONIANS. Another important set of laws was the Ten Commandments, given by Moses to the Israelites. The ANCIENT ROMANS had a fine legal system, on which much modern law is based. Today, not all countries have the same laws.

Above: The statue of Justice at the Old Bailey court, London. Below: The International Law Courts at the Hague, Netherlands.

Courts of Law

Courts are where cases are tried. A case may be about a criminal offence, such as stealing. Or it may be a civil offence, like a dispute between two business firms.

A court has a high seat for the JUDGE, or magistrate, tables and seats for LAWYERS and newspaper men, and seats for the public. If there is a prisoner, he stands inside a little enclosure called the dock. People who are connected with the case may be called to give evidence. They have to swear to tell the truth, and can be punished for not doing so.

Left: An old print of the inside of a criminal court in the nineteenth century.

Crime

Crime usually means breaking the law in a serious way. Murder (killing someone), assault (injuring someone), and stealing are crimes. A person who has committed a number of crimes is called a criminal. Parking a car in the wrong place is not a crime. It is an offence, however, and the motorist can be punished for it.

When a crime has been committed, the POLICE are mainly responsible for catching the criminal. They must catch the right person. It would be wrong to punish an innocent man who has done nothing. So the police must take the man they catch to COURT, and a magistrate – or a JUDGE and JURY – must decide whether he is innocent or guilty.

If he is guilty, a criminal can be sent to PRISON for a serious crime. If the crime is not serious, he can be fined (made to pay a sum of money). A criminal can also be put on probation. He will not be punished unless he commits another crime. A probation officer is put in charge of him.

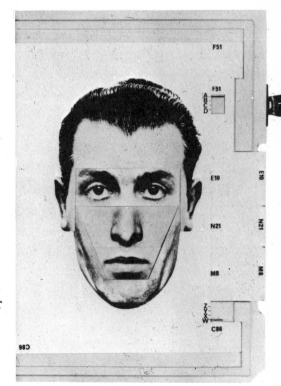

Above: A method of constructing the face of a criminal from parts of many different photographs.

Judge

A judge is a LAWYER who has worked for most of his life in the COURTS and knows the law thoroughly. He needs a very keen brain and must be fair to both sides.

In some countries, such as Britain and the United States, there is a JURY to help him, and he does not have to decide whether the prisoner is guilty or not. The jury settle guilt or innocence, but the judge helps them by explaining the law. He also sees that the trial is properly run, and sums up the main points before the jury decide. The judge fixes any punishment or sentence.

In civil cases (disputes that are not crimes) judges often decide the matter themselves without a jury.

Right: A British Lord Chancellor.
Far right: A French lawyer.

Jury

A jury is a group of men and women, usually twelve, who listen to a law case. They take a solemn oath to give an honest verdict or decision about what they think is the truth. They do not need to be experts in the law. The JUDGE helps them on legal points. They only have to decide what happened.

The first juries in England were in NORMAN times. Many countries have copied this system. In Britain, until recently, all twelve jurors had to agree before a verdict was reached, but now only ten have to agree. In the United States, all twelve have to reach the same decision. Otherwise there has to be a new trial, with different jurors.

In AUSTRALIA, in civil cases, there are sometimes only four people in a jury. In Scotland there may be as many as 15.

Lawyer

People who wish to become lawyers have to study the law for several years. Lawyers earn their living by advising people and speaking for them in the COURTS. The law is too complicated for most people to understand without help. In Britain there are two kinds of lawyer: a solicitor works mainly in his office and may speak only in the Magistrate's Court; a barrister's job is to speak in all kinds of courts. At present only a barrister may become a JUDGE.

In the United States the words are attorney and counsellor, but the same lawyer may do the work of both barrister and solicitor.

Justice of the Peace

A Justice of the Peace is also known in Britain as a magistrate. Magistrates are men and women who give up part of their time, without pay, to try cases in the local COURTS and to carry out certain other duties. Usually there are two present in the court. They may deal only with smaller CRIMES. More serious cases must go before a JUDGE. Magistrates are not usually LAWYERS, but they have one (the clerk) to help them. They also take short training courses in their duties. A few magistrates are full-time, paid lawyers.

In the United States, Justices of the Peace are local officials. In some states they are appointed by the governor. In other states they are elected. Their powers are similar to those of a British magistrate. In large cities the same job is done by POLICE magistrates.

Below left: A British Magistrate's Court. The magistrates are seated below the royal coat-of-arms. They are wearing ordinary clothes. A policeman is giving evidence from the witness box.

Police

The first duty of a police force is to see that people obey the law. But the police are not only concerned with catching criminals. They have to do such jobs as direct traffic, control crowds, find lost children, rescue people in danger, and give first aid in accidents. In many countries people often go to a policeman for help when they are in trouble.

Most policemen and policewomen wear UNI-FORMS. Those doing detective work often wear

Right: Policemen using Alsatian dogs in a search in Epping Forest, near London.
Below: A photograph of police in the nineteenth century. They were known as 'peelers' after their founder, Sir Robert Peel.

'plain' clothes, so that criminals will not know what they are. If a policeman sees a person actually committing a CRIME, he can arrest him on the spot. To make an arrest at other times he must get a court order called a warrant.

The police cannot try to punish people them-selves – they must take them to the COURTS. But in some countries, especially those ruled by a DICTATOR, there are secret police who arrest people who protest against the government.

Prisons

When a person has been tried, and is found guilty of a CRIME he may be sent to prison for a certain time. He may, however, be let out early if he behaves well. Sometimes people are put in prison while they are waiting for their trial.

Prisons used to be very harsh places where people were cruelly treated. In some countries they still are. But most civilized countries are trying to make prison a better place, where criminals can learn how to fit into an ordinary working life and live honestly when they come out. Today, there are many 'open' prisons, where certain prisoners are not kept locked up in cells, but have some freedom.

Police uniforms from different countries.
(1) Canadian Mounted Policeman. (2) British Police Sergeant. (3) Californian Motorcycle Patrolman. (4) French Traffic Policeman.
(5) Dutch Police Officer.

Strikes

A strike takes place when employees refuse to carry on working because they are dissatisfied with their pay or working conditions.

There are two kinds of strike – official and unofficial. Official strikes happen when the elected leaders of a Trade Union tell their members to stop work. Unofficial strikes take place when workers strike without the backing of their union officials.

Although strikes are common in EUROPE and America, they are still forbidden in many countries of the world.

(1) A strike at the Renault car company works in France. (2) Young men burning their draft cards on the steps of the Pentagon, during a demonstration against the Vietnam War. (3) The suffragettes had many clashes with police. (4) Student protest in South Africa. (5) Marchers protesting against unemployment in Britain, 1932. (6) Member of the Ulster Defence Association, Northern Ireland, 1972.

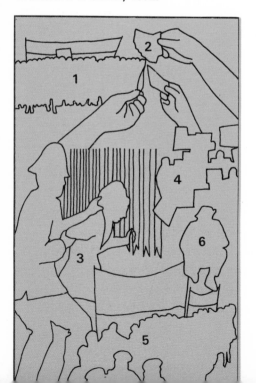

Demonstrations

Demonstrations occur when people feel strongly about something, and wish to protest. Sometimes demonstrators march through the streets, chanting and waving banners. Or they may simply sit down on the ground, and wait until they are moved by the POLICE.

Until recently most governments had no hesitation in using police or troops to break up demonstrations quite violently. Now, however, many demonstrations are peaceful.

Suffragettes

In the last century, many women began to feel that they should have the same rights as men. They felt particularly that they should have the right to vote at ELECTIONS.

The women's leaders were called 'suffragettes'. Susan B. Anthony in the U.S.A. and Emmeline Pankhurst in Britain were leading suffragettes. They realized that talking was getting them nowhere, and so they started a campaign of violence. Some chained themselves to railings, and others damaged public buildings.

This campaign had little effect on governments. After WORLD WAR I, however, women did get the vote, primarily as a result of their important work during the war.

Pacifists

Pacifists are men and women who refuse to fight because they believe that it is wrong to kill their fellow men. Some of the first pacifists were the QUAKERS, who were persecuted for their beliefs. Many other people have been pacifists. They have also been called conscientious objectors, which means that their conscience will not allow them to fight. During WORLD WAR I, all the warring nations severely punished pacifists.

Warfare is fighting between two or more countries, or between two parts of the same country. In the past, men have always fought wars, but the kind of war has changed from one age to another. New weapons have been important. The side which could produce a new weapon has often won. Even simple inventions like the stirrup have made great differences. Without stirrups it was very difficult to fight on horseback.

Sea warfare has its own history of change. So has the war in the air. War has become more complicated and more terrible as nations have become bigger and science has produced new weapons. Today, most people want to avoid war.

Above: A carving of an ancient battle from a Roman frieze.
Below: A scene from a film of the Battle of Waterloo.

Knights

Knights were heavily-armoured horsemen in the period called the Middle Ages (between about A.D. 450 and 1500). The King gave them lands and in return they had to be ready to fight for him and bring a number of men.

Knights lost their military usefulness when fire-arms were invented, and their ARMOUR could no longer protect them. In Britain, men are still made knights. This is now just an honour, or reward for something they have done.

This portrait of a knight, Sir John D'Abernon, was taken from his tomb. He died in 1277.

Castles

Castles began to be built in England and other parts of EUROPE about the time of WILLIAM THE CONQUEROR, who died in 1087.

At first castles were wooden towers on hills or huge piles of earth. Later castles were built of stone, and were much stronger. They had high walls round them with arrow-slits to shoot through. On the top of the wall were battlements, which had gaps for shooting and hurling rocks at the enemy. The walls had towers or bastions, and the main tower in the middle was called the keep. Outside the walls was a deep ditch or moat, often filled with water.

Most castles had a drawbridge, which could be pulled up to keep the enemy out. A heavy iron screen called a portcullis could be let down in front of the gates. The enemy might batter down the gates with a ram, climb the walls on long ladders, or just wait until the people inside ran out of food.

The remains of Caerphilly Castle, Wales. The castle is surrounded by water.

Crusades

The Crusades were wars fought by the Christian kings of EUROPE to capture JERUSALEM from the Moslem ARABS. The Arabs would not allow Christian pilgrims to visit the Holy places (the sites of events in the life of Jesus).

Crusaders wore a red cross as their badge. In 1099 they took Jerusalem, but the Saracen King Saladin recaptured it in 1187, and even Richard the Lion-Hearted could not drive him out. Crusades continued, off and on, for years. The Crusaders failed in their aims, but brought to Europe important knowledge from the scholars of the East.

Above: The Fourth Crusade was intended to capture Jerusalem. It ended, however, with the crusaders conquering Constantinople, shown here under attack.

Heraldry

When KNIGHTS rode to battle in ARMOUR, with helmets covering their faces, it was important to be able to tell who was who. Most people could not read, so they began to paint patterns on their shields in different colours. As there were thousands of different knights, they all had to be clearly marked out from the others. They made use of pictures to show who they were – perhaps a lion or a lily, a stag or a star or a wild boar's head.

Besides putting these on their shields, they had them embroidered on their coats, which gave us the word coat-of-arms. In time this coat-of-arms was also used on buildings, perhaps over a CASTLE gateway or in a CHURCH. There were strict rules on the design of coats-of-arms. The experts in the subject were the king's officers called heralds, so it is called heraldry.

Top: The Royal Coat-of-Arms of the United Kingdom.
Below: Two simple heraldic designs. A *chevron* (left) and a *pale* (right).

Civil Wars

Civil wars are fought between two sides in the same country, when people cannot agree peacefully. They have usually been even more cruel and savage than wars between different countries.

The English Civil War was between the King (Charles I) and his PARLIAMENT. They disagreed as to who should have the real power to govern. The King's followers were called Cavaliers and the Parliament men, Roundheads, because many of them wore their hair short. The war lasted from 1642 to 1646. Parliament, led by OLIVER CROMWELL, won, and the King was put to death.

Left: The English Civil War ended with the execution of King Charles I.

In the American Civil War (1861–1865) the northern states under President LINCOLN fought the southern states to keep the United States as one nation. The South wanted to break away and become a separate country so that they could keep slaves. The North won, but Lincoln was murdered in revenge.

The most famous modern civil war was fought in Spain from 1936 to 1939. General Franco and the ARMY successfully rose in revolt against the Republican Government.

There have been many other civil wars in history. In ancient ROME, JULIUS CAESAR fought Pompey. Caesar won but was murdered (44 B.C.), and a second war was fought by his killers, Brutus and Cassius, against Antony and Octavius. There were many other Roman civil wars between leaders seeking power for themselves.

Below left: A group of Union officers during the American Civil War.

Armies

The first battles were fought between small groups of men. Usually these men did not stay together for long. Military leaders found that they could keep a band of fighting men together, however, if they trained them well. They also needed good officers and enough food for their soldiers. The ANCIENT ROMANS organized an efficient army, with regiments called legions (4,000 to 6,000 men) and officers called centurions (in charge of 100 men).

An army includes infantry (foot soldiers), gunners (in charge of the ARTILLERY), and cavalry (soldiers on horseback).

Right: Jungle warfare. Modern weapons and uniforms are camouflaged so that they cannot easily be seen by an enemy.
Below: Soldiers of different ages. (1) Roman legionary. (2) Knight (fifteenth century). (3) French infantryman (1808). (4) German Infantryman (1916). (5) Modern United Nations soldier from Norway.

There must also be soldiers to bring up the food, build bridges, repair equipment, care for the wounded, and do other work to help the fighting men.

Until 200 years ago, armies were small (rarely more than a few thousand men). NAPOLEON started using all the men available to him, and armies became much bigger (100,000 men or more). In WORLD WAR I, some armies contained over a million men. Today wars are fought using machines, and the armies of some countries have become smaller again.

Most armies have officers to make decisions and lead the men. Non-commissioned officers (sergeants and corporals) are in charge of smaller groups of soldiers.

1   2

Above: Modern armies need to be able to move quickly from place to place. Here, a United States military hovercraft is being used in Vietnam. These craft can be used in very shallow water.

4   5

National Service

National service, or conscription, means that every fit young man must join the ARMY or serve his country in some way if he is 'called up' or 'drafted'. If the doctors find a man unfit, he is let off or 'exempted'.

Conscription was begun by NAPOLEON. He wanted to create big enough ARMIES to fight in his many campaigns. He also needed to replace the thousands of soldiers who were killed and wounded in his battles.

Many countries still have conscription, Britain had it only in the two World Wars and for some time afterwards. The United States abandoned the draft in 1973. As not all those available are needed, they are picked by ballot (at random).

Navies

A navy is made up of all the WARSHIPS of one country. Large navies are made up of several fleets. Each fleet is in a different part of the world (such as the PACIFIC Fleet). Fleets may have smaller divisions such as squadrons.

A modern fleet is made up of ships of various sizes and types – battleships, aircraft carriers, cruisers, destroyers, frigates, and submarines. Today, the new nuclear-powered submarines are one of the most important parts of a navy. They are able to remain under water for months.

Britain has had a navy since King Alfred's time, over 1000 years ago. For a century after NELSON, the British Navy was the biggest in the world and even its UNIFORM was imitated by others. In the last century, it claimed to keep the seas peaceful all over the globe. Now the biggest navies are those of the United States and the Soviet Union.

Above: The frigate U.S.S. *England* firing a missile. United States Navy frigates are larger than those of the British Navy.

Below: (1) Sailor, 1799. (2) Able Seaman, 1805. (3) Able Seaman, 1885. (4) French sailor, number one dress, 1915. (5) German Commander, 1939.

1   2   3   4   5

Air Forces

There were no air forces before WORLD WAR I. The first aircraft had just been invented – little 'flying machines' used for scouting (reconnaissance) and dropping small bombs.

The U.S. Air Force was formed in 1907. The British Royal Air Force, originally called the Royal Flying Corps, was formed in 1911. By 1918 the British Air Force alone had 22,000 powerful aircraft. After that, air forces grew more and more important.

In WORLD WAR II, aircraft were used to bomb enemy ports and FACTORIES. Most aircraft then were of two types – bombers and fighters. The fighter aircraft were faster and were used to protect the bombers on their own side and shoot down the enemy's. Today, long-range rockets, with powerful nuclear explosives in their warheads, may soon make bombers and fighters out of date.

Above: (1) Albatros D.V. (German), 1917. (2) Spitfire Mark IX (British), 1944. (3) F4B Phantom Jet (U.S. Navy). Below: R.A.F. Phantoms carrying rockets.

Below: A formation of Puma helicopters. These twin-engined aircraft were built jointly by France and Britain.

World War I

The Great War (as it used to be called) lasted from August 1914 to 11 November 1918. On one side were the two empires of GERMANY and Austria-Hungary, later joined by Bulgaria and TURKEY. They were called the Central Powers.

Against them were the Allies – that is, the Russian Empire to the east, the French to the west (who had promised to help the Russians), the British (who dared not let the Germans beat the French), and the Belgians (whose country was overrun by the Germans in the first few weeks). Later, the Italians, the Japanese, the United States, and many smaller nations joined the Allies. The war was fought on many different fronts.

After four years, the nations that had started the war were weary and exhausted. More than ten million soldiers had been killed. By coming fresh into the struggle, the United States tipped the scale, and the Central Powers collapsed in defeat.

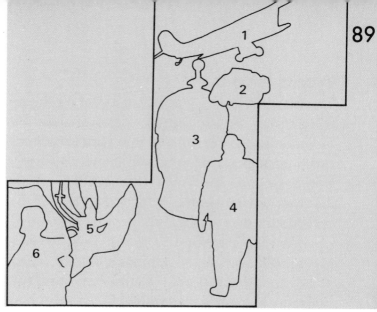

(1) Aircraft belonging to Baron M. von Richthofen (the Red Baron). (2) Tanks were introduced into the war in 1917. (3) Kaiser Wilhelm II, the German emperor. (4) Wounded Allied soldier. (5) U.S. recruiting symbol. (6) German war poster.

Red Cross

The Red Cross was started by a Swiss banker, Jean Henri Dunant, who was horrified by the sufferings of the troops wounded at the Battle of Solferino in 1859.

Until that time, ARMIES had few doctors and nurses, and soldiers often died where they fell. Dunant got a number of countries to make a Convention (agreement) at Geneva, promising not to shoot at Red Cross men who were not fighting but helping the wounded.

To show who they were, these men were to use the Red Cross flag. It was the exact opposite of the Swiss flag, which is a white cross on a red background. When Moslem countries took up the idea they did not want to use a Christian sign. They were allowed to use the Red Crescent.

Above: In peacetime the Red Cross do much social welfare work. They look after the old (above) and children (below).

World War II

The Second World War began largely because the German dictator, ADOLF HITLER, taught his followers in the Nazi Party that Germans were better than other peoples and should lead the world. He also wished to avenge the German defeat in WORLD WAR I.

He sent his soldiers to invade two small neighbouring countries (AUSTRIA and CZECHO-SLOVAKIA) and nobody stopped him. But when he attacked POLAND on 1 September 1939, the Poles fought back. The British and French had promised to help the Poles. The war began.

But Britain and FRANCE could not get their troops to Poland. They could only get ready to attack GERMANY from the west. They wanted

Allied leaders: (1) Winston Churchill. (3) Franklin D. Roosevelt. (5) General Eisenhower.
Axis leaders: (2) Adolf Hitler. (4) Japanese War Leader Tojo.
(6) Spitfire (British). (7) Stuka (German). (8) Tank (Soviet Union). (9) British infantry.

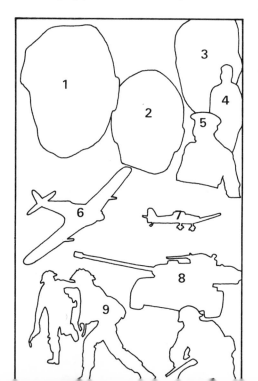

POLAND

CHOSLOVA...

IA HUNGARY

UGOS...

more time to prepare and did little fighting that winter. Meanwhile, Hitler conquered Poland.

Then he launched a surprise attack in the west, using bombers, parachute troops, and panzer (or armoured) columns of fast tanks. This method of fighting brought in a new word, *blitzkrieg*, meaning 'lightning war'.

First the Germans overran DENMARK and NORWAY, who had been 'neutral', not taking sides in the war. Then a second blitzkrieg was launched against the NETHERLANDS and BELGIUM, who were also neutral. Their lands were quickly overrun, and the Germans poured through into France. The French gave in, but the British Army escaped from the Dunkirk beaches of France in ships and boats. WINSTON CHURCHILL, the PRIME MINISTER, said Britain would fight on.

Hitler tried to break the spirit of the British with air raids, but he lost the Battle of Britain against the R.A.F. In 1941 he turned against Russia who had at first been on his side. But that country was too vast for him to conquer. The Russians had terrible losses but finally drove the Germans back.

Meanwhile, Hitler's allies had come into the war, the Italians under the Dictator MUSSOLINI and then JAPAN. On 7 December, 1941, the Japanese attacked the neutral United States fleet at Pearl Harbour and then conquered South-East ASIA.

By 1944 the tide was turning. The American, British, and other forces landed on the Normandy beaches (D-Day) and drove the Germans out of France. In 1945 they swept across Germany to meet their Russian allies. Germany surrendered. A few months later the first atomic bombs were dropped on Japan, Japan surrendered, and the war ended.

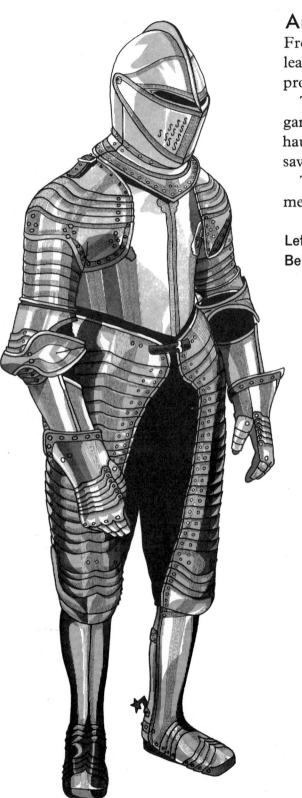

Armour

From the time of the ANCIENT EGYPTIANS (at least 1500 B.C.), soldiers have used armour to protect themselves in battle.

To protect their bodies, soldiers wore a strong garment which had many names – mail shirt, hauberk, breastplate or cuirass. The helmet saved them from blows on the head.

Today, the word 'armour' is often used to mean tanks.

Left: A suit of armour made for King Charles I.
Below: Heavily armoured Roman gladiator.

Swords

Swords are of many kinds, straight or curved, as short as the Roman type, or as long as the two-handed weapon of the Middle Ages. They might have sharp points for stabbing, keen edges for cutting, or both.

Western nations used straight swords until they met eastern enemies who preferred curved ones, like the Arab scimitar. Then they too began to use slightly curved swords called sabres, and these became the standard cavalry weapon until modern times, when machine-guns made swords and cavalry charges out of date.

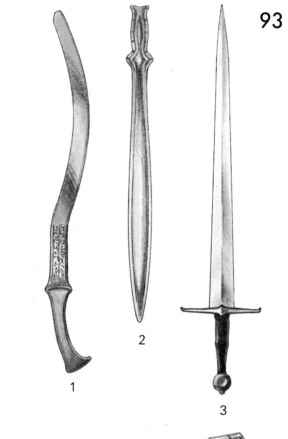

(1) Assyrian (twelfth century B.C.). (2) About 1000 B.C. (3) Cruciform (about 1400). (4) *Tachi* – Japanese ceremonial sword. (5) Swept hilt rapier (1600). (6) Falchion (1550). (7) Cup-hilted rapier (1640).

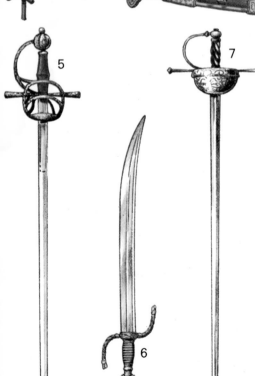

In NELSON's day, when sailors jumped aboard each others' ships and fought hand-to-hand, they also used a curved sword, called a cutlass. A rapier is quite the opposite, being thin and straight, with a point that can be covered safely for friendly FENCING.

The hilt of a sword is its handle. It may have a simple cross-piece or a curved guard over the whole hand. When not in use, the sword fits into a sheath or scabbard, and hangs from a belt or sash.

Brown Bess musket

12-bore shotgun

.303 rifle

Puckle revolving gun (1718)

Modern machine gun

84 mm anti-tank gun, with missile

Firearms and Artillery

Firearms were invented when men found that, if they exploded gunpowder at one end of a metal tube, it would send an iron or stone ball through the air with enough force to kill an enemy.

The first handguns (muskets) were used in 1364. They did not shoot far or straight. Then it was found that if the barrel had spiral grooves, the bullet went straighter. Guns with these barrels were called rifles.

Artillery now means big guns or rockets, but the word sometimes refers to the giant catapults (which threw rocks) and other machines that were used before gunpowder was invented. Cannon were first used about 1300.

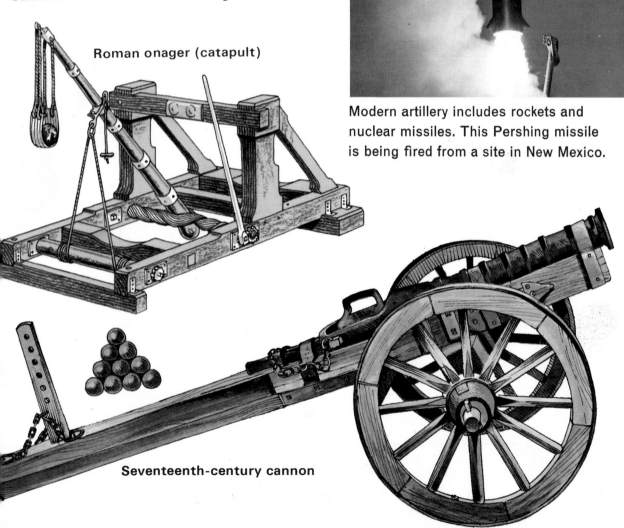

Modern artillery includes rockets and nuclear missiles. This Pershing missile is being fired from a site in New Mexico.

Roman onager (catapult)

Seventeenth-century cannon

MAN
FACTS AND FIGURES

OUR BODY. There are 206 bones in the human body. Everyone grows two sets of teeth (20 milk teeth that are lost in childhood, and 32 permanent teeth). The longest bone in the body is the femur, and the largest vein is the cardiac vein.

OUR HEALTH. Gold has long been used in dentistry: the Ancient Egyptians fixed loose teeth with gold wire. Not all bacteria are harmful: some aid digestion. The first operation under a general anesthetic took place in 1842 in the U.S.A.

PEOPLES OF THE WORLD. Today, there are more than 3500 million people in the world. It has been estimated that there will be twice that number by the year 2000. The most heavily populated country is China, with about 800 million inhabitants.

PEOPLES OF THE PAST. It is thought that man originated in eastern Africa. The population of Ancient Egypt was about 5 million — the same as modern Cairo. The Great Wall of China, man's largest construction, is nearly 2700 kilometres long.

RELIGIONS. Every year, 100,000 Moslems make a pilgrimage to Mecca, Mohammed's birth-place. More people follow Christianity than any other religion. In Judaism, a boy becomes a man at the age of 13 in a special ceremony called Bar Mitzvah.

FOLKLORE. The sphinx of Greek mythology ate people who could not answer its difficult riddle. An old legend describes how Faust sold his soul to the Devil in return for a longer life. In England, the last execution for witchcraft was in 1716.

GOVERNMENT. One of the oldest parliaments is the *Althing*, the parliament of Iceland, founded in A.D. 930. The first British prime minister was Sir Robert Walpole, who headed the government from 1721 to 1742. 132 countries are members of the United Nations.

LAW. The first country to abolish the death penalty was Liechtenstein in 1798; the first American states to do so were Michigan in 1846 and Wisconsin in 1853. During the nine days of the General Strike of 1926, $1\frac{1}{2}$ million British people stopped work.

WARFARE. Gunpowder was first used in the West in the thirteenth century. It was known even earlier in China. In World War II, about 55 million people were killed. The world's greatest bomb was a 57-megaton hydrogen bomb tested by U.S.S.R. in 1961.

VOLUME INDEX

PHOTO CREDITS

Australian News and Information Bureau, British Museum, British Red Cross, Canadian High Commission, Christian Science Publishing Society, Delaware State Bureau of Travel Development, Douglas Dickins F.R.P.S., E.E.C. London, Free China Centre, House of Representatives, Israel Government Tourist Office, Italian State Tourist Office, Japan Information Centre, Victor Kennett, London Hospital, Mansell Collection, Middle East Airlines, Moroccan Tourist Office, National Aeronautics and Space Administration, National Gallery London, National Portrait Gallery London, Netherlands Tourist Office, New Scotland Yard, Olympic Airways, Outlook Films Ltd., Jacques Penry, Radio Times Hulton Picture Library, Religious Society of Friends, St. Bartholomew's Hospital, Smithsonian Institution, South African Tourist Corporation, South Dakota Department of Highways, State of Minnesota Department of Economic Development, Tate Gallery London, United Kingdom Atomic Energy Authority, United Nations, United States Embassy, University College Hospital Dental School, Robert Updegraff, Warner Columbia, Watch Tower Bible Tract Society, Westminster Hospital. The photograph of Caerphilly Castle on page 81 is British Crown Copyright, reproduced by permission of the Controller of Her Britannic Majesty's Stationery Office.